W9-BGJ-813

THE LAP-BAND™
SOLUTION

A partnership in weight loss
An information book

Revised edition

Paul O'Brien MD

Centre for Bariatric Surgery, Australia
and
American Institute of Gastric Banding, USA

Melbourne University Publishing

MUP CUSTOM
An imprint of Melbourne University Publishing Ltd
187 Grattan Street, Carlton, Victoria 3053, Australia
mup-custom@unimelb.edu.au
www.mup.com.au

First published 2007
Reprinted in 2008, 2010

Revised edition published 2011
Text © Paul O'Brien 2011
Images © individual copyright holders 2011
Design and typography © Melbourne University Publishing Ltd 2011

Typeset by Sonya Murphy/Typeskill
Cover design by Design by Committee
Printed in Australia by Griffin Press

National Library of Australia Cataloguing-in-Publication entry

O'Brien, Paul (Paul Edmond), 1943–
The lap-band solution : a partnership in weight loss / Paul O'Brien.
Rev ed.

ISBN: 9780522858853 (pbk.)

Includes bibliographical references and index.

Obesity—Surgery.
Stomach—Surgery.
Weight loss—Surgery.

617.43

CONTENTS

FOREWORD TO THE REVISED EDITION

In the 4 years since Dr O'Brien wrote the first edition of *The LAP-BAND™ Solution*, we have seen a remarkable growth in the number of people who have had the LAP-BAND™ procedure. Since its introduction in 2001, the LAP-BAND™ has become the most commonly performed weight-loss surgery in the US. The reasons are fairly straightforward. It is the safest weight-loss procedure, it is adjustable, and it is reversible. I have had the privilege of working closely with Dr O'Brien as he has generously shared his knowledge and expertise with bariatric surgeons throughout the world. As the world's foremost authority on the LAP-BAND™, his research has been a key component in the phenomenal growth of this life-saving procedure.

Perhaps the most dramatic change regarding the LAP-BAND™ has been the widespread adoption of day surgery for its placement. Weight-loss surgery used to involve a multi-day hospital stay with all the risks, cost and inconvenience that three days in a hospital entails. Now, thanks to advances in technique, LAP-BAND™ patients routinely have their procedure done in the morning and then relax in their own homes by the afternoon.

The company I founded has, through our affiliated doctors and surgery centers, performed over 20,000 LAP-BAND™ procedures. Our success has been made possible by the lessons we learned from the pioneering work done by Dr O'Brien. The most important lesson has been the importance of an integrated, effective aftercare program. The effectiveness of any weight-loss procedure is determined largely by what happens after the procedure. The LAP-BAND™, with its unique ability to be adjusted to the patients' exact needs, allows patients to achieve long-term sustainable weight loss.

This book will be your owner's manual and road map as you begin your journey to a healthier, happier lifestyle. With this book as your guide, your trip will be a successful one.

Peter R. Gottlieb
Executive Chairman
True Results
The American Institute of Gastric Banding

January 2011

FOREWORD TO THE FIRST EDITION

When Dr O'Brien first told me of his plans to write a book about the LAP-BAND™, I was delighted. Not only is he a gifted surgeon and the world's foremost authority, but a compassionate, kind man who genuinely cares about the health and welfare of people struggling with their weight.

You, the reader, are to be commended for taking the initiative to learn more about the remarkable LAP-BAND™ system and how this simple device can change your life. Whether you are considering having the procedure or already have the band and want to optimize your success, this book provides the information you need in a clear and concise manner.

Those of us involved with LAP-BAND™ surgery in the US have always looked to our colleagues in Australia because of their much longer experience with the procedure, as well as the outstanding weight loss achieved by their patients. As I spoke with Dr O'Brien and observed his interaction with his patients, the importance of a structured aftercare program became clearly apparent. I encourage you to look at the LAP-BAND™ as a tool—remarkable, yes, but still a tool. The key to success with any tool is understanding how it works and the things you as a patient can do to make it work better for *you*.

This book will serve as an owner's manual and road map as you begin your journey to a happier, healthier lifestyle. Best of luck and enjoy the trip.

Peter R. Gottlieb
Founder and Director
The American Institute of Gastric Banding

ABOUT THE AUTHOR

 Paul O'Brien is a world leader in the LAP-BAND™ procedure. He was one of its originators, having been involved in its design and testing in the early 1990s, and he placed the first LAP-BAND™ in Australia in 1994. He heads the Centre for Bariatric Surgery (CBS), a major clinical center for the assessment and treatment of obesity in Melbourne, Australia (www.lapbandaustralia.com.au). The center has seven surgeons and many physicians and other health professionals committed to providing a safe and effective weight-loss program. By the end of 2010, they had treated more than 6,000 people with the LAP-BAND™.

He is also Emeritus Professor of Surgery at Monash University and the Emeritus Director of the Centre for Obesity Research and Education (CORE), a major research center within Monash University in Melbourne (www.core.monash.org). His principal areas of clinical and research interest are in the morbidity of obesity and the health benefits of weight loss. He has published more than 250 research papers in the medical literature and has been active in conducting numerous postgraduate courses and workshops on obesity and its treatments in Australia, the US, countries of the Asia–Pacific region, South America and Canada.

He is Past President of the Obesity Surgery Society of Australia and New Zealand (1997–2004). He was President of the 11th World Congress of the International Federation for the Surgery of Obesity (IFSO), held in Sydney, Australia in 2006.

He has been National Medical Director for the American Institute of Gastric Banding (AIGB), in Dallas, Texas (www.aigb.com) since 2006. AIGB is the most active and experienced clinical group in the US for providing the LAP-BAND™ in a day surgery setting, and through their True Results clinics (www.trueresults.com) more than 20,000 patients have been treated.

He lives in Melbourne with his wife, Eve, and near their four grown-up children Tim, Charlotte, Richard and Anna.

ACKNOWLEDGMENTS

I would like to thank our patients who, by telling us how they feel, have taught us so much. They have been so keen, so supportive and so tolerant. Hopefully we have been able to contribute to their health and happiness as a result.

The staff of the Centre for Bariatric Surgery have been invaluable in working together to find the optimal program of care. In particular, Chris Halkett, one of our Nurse Coordinators, has worked closely with me since we began the program in 1994, and knows our patients better than I, providing advice and reassurance for them day and night.

I am very grateful to the other surgeons of the group — Drs Wendy Brown, Stewart Skinner, Stephen Blamey, Gary Crosthwaite, Andrew Smith and Paul Burton — for their skilful support and commitment to excellent patient care.

Our medical aftercare team began when Dr Audrey Kotzander joined me in 1997 and now also includes Drs Anna Korin, Peter Baquie, Paul MacCartney, Kathryn De Garis, Karina Solyarsky, Caroline Lloyd and Samantha Green as Primary Care Practitioners, and Linda Schachter, Stuart Moir and John Wentworth as Specialist Physicians. Much of our understanding of aftercare needs has been developed from discussions with these colleagues.

Cheryl Laurie, Robyn Bowyer, Julie Playfair and Eve O'Brien provide the nursing support and collect great insights through their close contact with our patients. Helen Bauzon is our dietician and has a unique understanding of the banded patient's needs. Margaret Anderson has maintained the database that is central to the aftercare of our patients, tracking their progress and measuring their outcomes.

Through the Centre for Obesity Research and Education (CORE) we have observed, measured, analyzed and studied many aspects of the problems of obesity, and the benefits of weight loss and the LAP-BAND™ process. Many have contributed to these studies over the years, including Wendy Brown, the current director of CORE, assisted by Paul Burton and Leah Brennan who supervise an energetic and committed group of researchers.

A key feature of successful LAP-BAND™ practice is the coordinated involvement of a multidisciplinary team, and the successful patient outcomes of the Centre for Bariatric Surgery are a credit to the entire team.

I thank my wife Eve, who has tolerated my commitment to the study of obesity and the care of the obese, my frequent travel, and my obsessive involvement in research and clinical practice. She gently murmurs to me that it is time to retire, but it is too much fun doing something that works so well. I pretend I do not hear.

INTRODUCTION

This book has been written for two groups of people. Firstly, it is written for those people who have a problem with their weight and want to be informed about the LAP-BAND™ as one of the major options for treatment.

Secondly, it is written for the people who have made the decision to proceed with the LAP-BAND™ procedure and need to know what will happen at the time of surgery, what are the guidelines for eating, exercise and lifestyle, and how they can contribute to achieving an optimal outcome.

It is not necessary to read the book from cover to cover. You can if you wish but that is not our expectation. Please read the key parts at different stages of your progress, from initially exploring the possibility of having the LAP-BAND™ through to the first days, months and years after it is placed, and as you learn a new way of life. Over the years after the surgery, read the chapters on eating and exercise again and again to be sure you are fully familiar with them and are following the advice.

The first two chapters provide background information about the problem of obesity and the benefits of weight loss. Many people who come to see us are already well informed on these matters. It may be that much of the material in these two chapters is already known to you. But please look through it. See if there is new information. See if the information presented gives you a better understanding of your problem and your options. The decision to have the LAP-BAND™ is one of the most important healthcare decisions that you will make and it is best to make that decision on the basis of good information and understanding. These two chapters are there to provide that information.

Chapter 3 reviews the options available to you if you have the disease of obesity. It is an overview rather than a detailed review of treatments. We give enough information about each of the treatment options to clarify why we do or do not expect that treatment to be your best option. For someone who is starting the process of exploring the treatments available for weight reduction, this chapter should be helpful. It does not attempt to provide a comprehensive review of all the other surgical options. That is for others to provide. It rather focuses on why we see the LAP-BAND™ as the best option for the primary treatment of the disease of obesity.

Chapter 4 is new to this revised edition, and explains how the band works for you and how you can work with the band to optimize your weight loss. The information in this chapter explains the difference between "satiety" and "satiation," and how learning to recognize the signals of each is important to help you eat correctly, and to work with your doctor in partnership to ensure correct adjustment of the band.

Chapter 5 provides detailed information about the LAP-BAND™. It covers the key advantages of the LAP-BAND™ over other options. It reviews the good outcomes and the possible bad outcomes. It ends with a synthesis of the attributes of all the other possible treatments for obesity in comparison with the LAP-BAND™.

Chapter 6 and the chapters that follow it are for you once you have decided to go ahead with the LAP-BAND™. This chapter tells you what you need to know about your time in hospital and the first 4 weeks after operation. By that time, you will be over the operation, the band will be settling into position and you will be ready to start the phase of serious weight reduction.

Chapters 7 and 8 provide details of the rules and guide-lines relating to eating, drinking, exercise and activity that are recommended when you have the LAP-BAND™. These are the two most important chapters in the book. We want you to read them carefully and read them several times if you are planning to go ahead with the procedure.

Chapter 9 informs you about the adjustment sequence. It explains how we determine when to add fluid, how much to add, and what happens to your appetite in association with adjustments. The adjustability of the band is its most important attribute. We use it with enthusiasm but with careful judgment.

Chapter 10 tells you what should happen with your weight as we adjust the band and as you follow the eating and exercise guidelines. It tells you how much weight you are most likely to lose, how quickly you should lose it, what we do if you are losing weight more slowly than we expected, and tells you more about what you can do to optimize the effectiveness of the band.

Chapter 11 summarizes the guidelines into eight golden rules. We encourage you to treat those rules as critical to achieving the best possible result from the LAP-BAND™.

They are so important that this revised edition of *The LAP-BAND™ Solution* also comes with a DVD of "The Eight Golden Rules." There are animations on the DVD of how the band works that will greatly assist your understanding of why you must follow the eight golden rules.

Chapter 12 addresses the many questions that are put to us. Many of the answers repeat parts of the earlier chapters, but these questions are gathered here for your convenience, as they do represent what we know people worry about. The chapter is well worth reading, as some of these questions that others have asked you may not have thought about yourself, but will nevertheless find that you are keen to know the answers to them.

Please read the parts that are relevant to you at the particular time. Feel free to roam through the various areas and return to some to read again and again. The book is designed to help you understand your part of the partnership. The LAP-BAND™ is highly successful when that partnership is in place. We hope that the book helps you to achieve your share of the safe, gentle and successful weight loss that is unique to the LAP-BAND™.

THE PROBLEM OF OBESITY

KEY POINTS

1 Obesity is the most common health problem in our community.

2 Obesity causes many diseases and markedly increases the risk of dying prematurely.

3 Obesity reduces quality of life by limiting physical activity and encouraging social isolation.

4 The costs of obesity through increased health costs and reduced effectiveness in the community are very high.

5 The body mass index or BMI is the best simple method for measuring how obese someone is.

CHAPTER 1

OBESITY IN TODAY'S SOCIETY

Obesity is rapidly becoming one of the greatest health challenges of the 21st century.[1] No disease is more common and causes more unnecessary illness or early death than obesity. Furthermore, there is no other single problem that so reduces the quality of life or increases the demand for health-care services.

The problem is worldwide. In the US, more than two out of every three adults are overweight and about one in three is obese. This means that approximately 60 million people have the disease of obesity in the US alone. More than one in five Australian adults, an estimated 3.7 million of a population of 20 million, is obese. For both countries, the incidence of obesity has doubled since 1980. Alarmingly, obesity starts in child-hood, and already 7% of our teenagers are obese.

Around the world, all countries have a growing problem. There are now an estimated 300 million people world-wide who are suffering from obesity and its con-sequences. In both developed and developing nations, we see a similar pattern. In Russia, 54% of adults are overweight. In Brazil, the figure is 36%, and in Malaysia, 27%. Even China has a developing problem. A recent survey of adults in urban Shanghai reported that 29.5% were overweight and 4.3% were obese.

After millions of years of evolution we carry a genetic structure designed to enable us to survive the life of the hunter–gatherer; and our health and our lives are now threatened by a lifestyle characterized by ready access to copious amounts of attractive food and very little need for physical activity. Foods high in fat, carbohydrates and, in particular, simple sugars are booming. The US Department of Agriculture reports that the US per capita intake of sugar was 152.4 lb (69 kg) in 2000. This is equal to nearly half a pound (230 g) of sugar per person each day. Most will claim they are not eating that much sugar. We would all be surprised to see that sugar is now a part of so many foods that we don't even realize we are eating sugar. It has infiltrated our diet to a frightening extent. One hundred years ago, the sugar intake per capita was only 0.5 lb (230 g). Is it any wonder that we have a problem?

And we don't even need to get out of the chair to order the food to be delivered or to change the channels on the television. Activity has become optional. The combination of increased intake of energy and reduced energy expenditure inevitably leads to progressive weight increase.

DEFINING AND MEASURING OBESITY

Obesity is a disease in which fat has accumulated to the extent that health is impaired.

Note that there are three key components to this definition:

1   **"Obesity is a disease ..."** It is only recently that major health authorities such as the World Health Organization and the US Federal Department of Health have acknowledged obesity as a disease. This change is most important as the disease of obesity can now begin to claim attention and an allocation of resources as do all other diseases.

2   **"... in which fat has accumulated ..."** Fat is the key element of obesity. Primarily we are interested in how much fat there is in the body. We are not focused on weight per se. However, as we do not have a simple office method for directly measuring the fat content of the body, we have to use surrogate measures. We could use weight alone but this would be terribly misleading. The tall person is always likely to be heavier than the shorter person. Therefore, at a minimum, we have to take height into account as well. Currently, our best way to do this is by using the body mass index or the BMI. We will discuss how we calculate the BMI and look at its strengths and weaknesses below.

3   **"... to the extent that health is impaired."** We are
dealing with a disease that causes disease. The disease of obesity may express itself in various ways.
It may be expressed as type 2 diabetes or as any of
the dozens of known diseases that are caused by or
made worse by obesity. It may be expressed as a
physical or psychosocial limitation on the quality of
your life. For example, you may no longer be able to
do the things that are normally expected. Your self-
esteem or self-confidence may be severely lowered,
leading to isolation, depression or unemployment. Or
it may be expressed as a risk to your future health.
You may feel fine now but you are aware that you are
at high risk of disease in the future and that your life
expectancy is being reduced by your obesity.

We will look at the disease of obesity in more detail
below but, firstly, let's be clear about how we measure
this disease.

THE BODY MASS INDEX (BMI)

The BMI is our best single measure of obesity.

The BMI is a measure that combines the weight and
the height according to the following formula:

BMI = weight (in pounds) divided by height^2 (in inches) × 705

or

BMI = weight (in kilograms) divided by height^2 (in meters)

We use BMI as our primary measure of obesity. We want a measure that is simple to make and acceptably accurate. Direct measure of the amount of fat in the body is not simple and measuring weight alone is not accurate enough. Across the world, the BMI is accepted as the best primary measure because, in most situations, it provides an accurate reflection of the amount of fat present. As weight increases, it is mainly as fat. There may be some increase in muscle mass as well but it is usually small in proportion. As you lose weight, the loss of fat is predominant but you may also lose some muscle mass.

We have now established what we consider are normal and abnormal levels of BMI. The BMI values for Western populations are shown in Table 1.1.

TABLE 1.1 BMI VALUES FOR WESTERN POPULATIONS

Label	BMI	Label	BMI
Normal	18.5–25	Severely obese	>35
Overweight	25–30	Morbidly obese	>40
Obese	>30	Super obese	>50

Any level of obesity is bad for you. At a BMI of 30 you are at a higher risk of disease and have a reduced life expectancy. For most people, quality of life is reduced. At progressively higher levels of BMI the likelihood of disease increases, the risk to life is greater and the quality of life is lower. Of course, there is much variation between individuals. Some people can have quite a high BMI and not recognize any problem. Others can be mildly obese and yet suffer significantly.

If the concept of BMI is confusing to you, Tables 1.2 and 1.3 show the BMI for different weights and heights, in US units and in metric units, respectively.

TABLE 1.2 BODY MASS INDEX CHART—US UNITS

Weight (lb)	Height (in)								
	60	62	64	66	68	70	72	74	76
120	23	22	21	19	18	17	16	15	15
130	25	24	22	21	20	19	18	17	16
140	27	26	24	23	21	20	19	18	17
150	29	27	26	24	23	22	20	19	18
160	31	29	28	26	24	23	22	21	20
170	33	31	29	27	26	24	23	22	21
180	35	33	31	29	27	26	24	23	22
190	37	35	33	31	29	27	26	24	23
200	39	37	34	32	30	29	27	26	24
210	41	38	36	34	32	30	29	27	26
220	43	40	38	36	34	32	30	28	27
230	45	42	40	37	35	33	31	30	28
240	47	44	41	39	37	35	33	31	29
250	49	46	43	40	38	36	34	32	30
260	51	48	45	42	40	38	36	34	32
270	53	49	46	44	41	39	37	35	33
280	55	51	48	45	43	40	38	36	34
290	57	53	50	47	44	42	39	37	35
300	59	55	52	49	46	43	41	39	37
320	63	59	55	52	48	46	43	41	40
340	66	62	58	55	52	49	46	44	41
360	70	66	62	58	55	52	49	46	44
380	74	70	65	61	58	55	52	49	46
400	78	73	69	65	61	57	54	51	49

TABLE 1.3 BODY MASS INDEX CHART—METRIC UNITS

Weight (kg)	Height (cm)								
	152	158	163	168	173	178	183	188	193
54	23	22	21	19	18	17	16	15	15
59	25	24	22	21	20	19	18	17	16
64	27	26	24	23	21	20	19	18	17
68	29	27	26	24	23	22	20	19	18
73	31	29	28	26	24	23	22	21	20
77	33	31	29	27	26	24	23	22	21
82	35	33	31	29	27	26	24	23	22
86	37	35	33	31	29	27	26	24	23
91	39	37	34	32	30	29	27	26	24
95	41	38	36	34	32	30	29	27	26
100	43	40	38	36	34	32	30	28	27
104	45	42	40	37	35	33	31	30	28
109	47	44	41	39	37	35	33	31	29
113	49	46	43	40	38	36	34	32	30
118	51	48	45	42	40	38	36	34	32
123	53	49	46	44	41	39	37	35	33
127	55	51	48	45	43	40	38	36	34
132	57	53	50	47	44	42	39	37	35
136	59	55	52	49	46	43	41	39	37
145	63	59	55	52	48	46	43	41	40
154	66	62	58	55	52	49	46	44	41
163	70	66	62	58	55	52	49	46	44
172	74	70	65	61	58	55	52	49	46
181	78	73	69	65	61	57	54	51	49

It is important to understand that BMI is not a perfect measure. It is a surrogate for measuring the amount of fat. Its great advantage is that it is simple to measure and it is generally accurate enough. However, it can be misleading. Below are four examples that demonstrate that BMI is not a perfect measure.

Firstly, the critical cutoff of BMI for obesity is different for some ethnic groups. For people who originated from European countries, the so-called Western world, a BMI of 30 is considered the dividing line between being overweight and obese. But, from careful study of the amount of fat in the body at different weights, we now know that Chinese, Indian and Malay populations should be regarded as obese at BMI levels of 27–28 rather than 30 because at any given weight they will have a higher proportion of fat. As a more detailed picture of the ethnic differences emerges we may find other groups who should have different cutoffs also.

Secondly, the athlete who builds up muscle through heavy training can put on weight without additional fat. BMI measures in such a person will not reflect the fat content of the body. There are many examples of bodybuilders or football players who have a high BMI but very little body fat. They are not obese as they do not have an abnormal accumulation of fat. As long as we understand that BMI is not a direct but a surrogate measure for fat, we should not be confused by this exception.

Thirdly, the BMI does not tell us anything about the distribution of fat, and yet we recognize that those with "central" obesity—the big belly—have a higher risk of a range of obesity-related disorders, such as heart disease and diabetes, compared to those with "peripheral" obesity—big bottom and legs. In other words, the "apple" shape is worse than the "pear" shape. Again, simple observation and measurement enable us to avoid confusion on this.

Finally, the accumulation of excess fat in children and adolescents is not adequately reflected by measuring height and weight alone. We must include age and then look at growth and weight charts to see if the child is outside the expected range.

While we should recognize these potential pitfalls, BMI remains our best general measure. It is used throughout the world, it is easy to measure and to understand, and is now established as the appropriate starting point for describing obesity.

OTHER MEASURES OF FATNESS

Although the BMI is the most commonly used and most simple method for estimating the amount of fat in the body as a proportion of total body weight, we can do this more accurately with some relatively sophisticated tests such as DEXA and underwater weighing.

DEXA

DEXA is now a common test and potentially very useful in measuring fatness and following the loss of fat as weight decreases. DEXA stands for dual energy X-ray absorptiometry. Up to now it has been used mainly for measuring the density of bones to check for possible thinning of the bones or osteoporosis. The DEXA machine looks a bit like a CT scanner but uses much lower energy and therefore has less potential for harm. It is too complex to use on a day-to-day basis but does tell us exactly how much fat is in the body and can be used intermittently to monitor progress.

Underwater weighing

Underwater weighing is an accurate way to measure the fat content of the body. It provides a simple measure of weight per unit volume and takes us back to Ancient Greece and to Archimedes lying in his bath. He is said to have shouted "Eureka!" when he realized how, through the displacement of water, he could discover if the King's golden crown contained some base metals. In this same way, we can now discover how much of you is fat. However, although it is accurate and therefore valuable in research studies, it is not really acceptable for most people and not suitable for frequent measuring.

Bioimpedance

Bioimpedance, otherwise called BIA, is well known, commonly used and therefore deserves comment. You can readily buy scales that provide measures of bioimpedance and these scales give a readout of total body fat. You will see them advertised by commercial weight-loss groups, and physicians' offices frequently have them. More complex devices are also available.

The concept is that a small electrical current is passed across the body and the resistance to the flow of that current is measured. Fat impedes the flow of the current more than other body tissue and, from the measurement of this impedance, the instrument uses a formula to calculate how much of the body is fat. Unfortunately, the technique is not an accurate measure of fatness. Because of the way the calculations are performed by these devices, we are able to get just as accurate a measure of the amount of fat by using the BMI alone. Don't be fooled by the fact that it prints out numbers or sounds highly scientific. It is not.

THE PROBLEMS THAT OBESITY CAUSES

1 REDUCED LIFE EXPECTANCY

The first problem of obesity to focus on is the one that many obese people think about the least—you are less likely to live a long life if you are too fat. Life insurance companies have known this for a long time. They know that the fatter you are the worse risk you are to them.

The graph in Figure 1.1 shows the risk of dying in a large group of American men and women who were followed for many years. The relative risk of dying is set at 100 for normal weight and the graph shows how your risk increases progressively as you move above a BMI of 27.

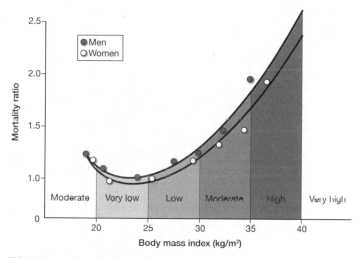

FIGURE 1.1 BMI AND THE RISK OF DEATH

If your BMI is greater than 35, you are in the high-risk group and, by the time you reach a BMI of 40, the risk is nearly three times that of people who have normal weight. The risk rises very steeply as your weight goes above a BMI of 40.

The Centers for Disease Control in Atlanta, Georgia, estimated that, depending on how you calculate the numbers, there were between 112,000 and 380,000 excess deaths from obesity-related disease in the US during the year 2000.[2,3] Whichever figure is correct, it is a horrific statistic, far worse than road deaths (43,000) or terrorism (0) for that year. Even the young are paying a price for their obesity. Teenagers entering adulthood

with a BMI greater than 40 would have their life expectancy reduced by up to 13 years for a male and 8 years for a female. That is a major part of their life lost before they are even adults. The risk of early death from obesity is similar to the risk from smoking.

2 MEDICAL DISEASES

A pathogen is something that causes disease. Obesity is the consummate pathogen. It causes or makes worse a broad range of diseases, such as type 2 diabetes, coronary heart disease and stroke, hypertension, sleep apnea, depression, a range of cancers including breast, gynecological and gastrointestinal malignancies, abnormal levels of fats in the blood, polycystic ovary syndrome, inflammation of the liver, and osteoarthritis of the lower spine and joints that bear your weight, such as the hips, knees and feet.

Also, obese people are more at risk of accidents at work, at home or on the road, and are more likely to suffer sudden unexplained death.

There is a long list of illnesses that are either caused by obesity or are made worse by obesity. The ones that are listed in Table 1.4 are the common and most important of such illnesses.

We will discuss a number of these diseases in Chapter 2, where we also look at the improvements in health that occur with weight loss. For now, we will look at some of the physical, social and economic problems that come with obesity.

3 PHYSICAL LIMITATIONS

Morbidly obese people often cannot do the things that others can do. Sporting activities are generally out, which excludes them from many family pastimes. Physical activity of any sort can be quite difficult due to shortness of breath or just plain tiredness, so that even housework or standard employment is a challenge.

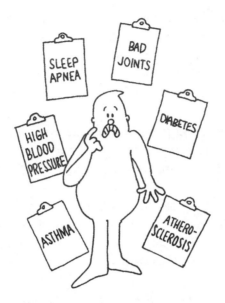

TABLE 1.4 ILLNESSES CAUSED BY OR EXACERBATED BY OBESITY

- Diabetes
- Hypertension
- Dyslipidemia
- Ischemic heart disease
- Cardiomyopathy
- Pulmonary hypertension
- Asthma
- Hypoventilation syndromes
- Obstructive sleep apnea
- Gallstones
- Non-alcoholic steatohepatitis (NASH)
- Urinary incontinence
- Gastroesophageal reflux
- Arthritis—weight bearing
- Lower back pain
- Infertility
- Polycystic ovarian syndrome
- Obstetric complications
- Deep vein thrombosis and thromboembolism
- Depression
- Immobility
- Breast, gastrointestinal, prostate and endometrial cancer
- Venous/stasis ulcers
- Intertrigo
- Accident-prone

Most morbidly obese people cannot buy clothes easily and some have difficulty getting into and out of cars, or into seats on public transport or at the theatre.

Airplane travel can be a major embarrassment. You may need to ask for an extension for the seat belt. You may not be able to lower the table. You may see the person allocated the seat next to you go to the flight attendant and ask for another seat. Just the thought of these things happening can put you off travel.

Flexibility is reduced. The toes get progressively out of reach or even out of sight, making cutting the toenails a shared responsibility. Personal hygiene becomes a problem if you cannot get the toilet paper or the towel to reach all the nooks and crannies.

4 SOCIAL ISOLATION

Many people who are morbidly obese feel uncomfortable in public. Often they sense that other people
are looking at them and commenting on their weight
and the difficulties it produces in dressing well and
moving easily. They prefer to withdraw—to live within
the family circle at home, rarely venturing into the
public gaze.

This may help them cope with embarrassment but
equally it deprives them of the chance to work, to
join the family in outside activities and to join friends
socially. It is not surprising, therefore, to find that the
morbidly obese have a low level of self-esteem and a
feeling of worthlessness and uselessness. It is common
for obese people to suffer depression. They hate their
appearance. They feel that they are unattractive to their
partner or children and to others.

Obese people suffer social bias, prejudice and discrimination as a result of their appearance. Society stig-
matizes the obese. Obesity is probably the only area
left where discrimination is still considered acceptable.
Unfavorable remarks about someone because of their
sex, race or disability are not acceptable in our society
today, and rightly so. However, unfavorable remarks
about someone's obesity are still okay. This attitude
is implanted early. When children are shown the

silhouette of an obese person they describe the person as ugly, smelly, dirty, lazy, stupid, dishonest, weak-willed, awkward, a liar and a cheat.

5 ECONOMIC CONSIDERATIONS

Obesity costs the community a great deal in view of the high healthcare needs of the obese.[1] These costs consist of both the direct costs of investigating and treating obesity-related diseases, such as physician visits, tests, medicine and hospitalizations, and

My patients are the best witnesses to the problems of the obese. The following is a list of their anecdotes about things that have happened to them because of their obesity:

- Waiting in the queue at the supermarket with a trolley of shopping and a stranger looking into the trolley and pointing to items saying, "Someone your size shouldn't be eating that."
- Walking down the street and a small child speaking in a really loud voice saying "Mommy, look at that big fat lady. She's the fattest lady I've ever seen." Others all turn to look at me.
- Walking along the street and a carload of young men/louts yelling obscenities to me about my size.
- In a nightclub, overhearing a man refer to me as a "beached whale."
- Traveling in Asia and being constantly harassed by locals about my size. There were some very cruel comments and frequent attempts to touch and squeeze parts of my body.
- At an airport, a very loud and public scene with an official saying I was so fat that I had to pay for two seats on the airplane.
- On an airplane trip, being very publicly moved to another seat, the flight attendant saying that I was "too heavy" and they "need to balance up the weight on the plane."
- Walking into a dress shop and being told rudely that "there is nothing to fit you here."
- When shopping, being often totally ignored while other customers receive attention. (This difficulty in clothing shops we hear about again and again. And when they have lost weight, they are greeted warmly and asked if they need any help.)
- Staff checking that the chair in a restaurant is strong enough to hold me, pretending to be anxious that I may break it.
- Getting into an elevator and a woman already inside saying to her child as she looked directly at me, "I think we'll get out here and wait for the next elevator."

indirect costs, such as earnings lost because of illness or disability or the loss of future earnings because of premature death. In the US, these costs were estimated by the US Department of Health and Human Services to be $117 billion for the year 2000. This was made up of $61 billion for direct costs and $56 billion for indirect costs. Major contributors to this total cost are heart disease ($9 billion), osteoarthritis ($21 billion), high blood pressure ($4 billion), gallbladder disease ($3 billion), and cancers of the breast, uterus and colon (alone $7 billion). The number of annual workdays lost was nearly 40 million. It was estimated that, in the year 2000 in the US, people made 63 million visits to their physician because of obesity-related problems.

Whichever way you look at these numbers, we are spending a great deal on obesity. If these costs could be reduced by weight loss, it would pay for a lot of treatments.

SUMMARY

Obesity is one heck of a problem. It is the worst cause of disease in the Western world. It leads to early death in more people than almost any other cause. What life you do have is severely reduced in quality because of the physical and social problems generated by the disease. And it costs us as a community a great deal of money because of the direct and indirect effects of the health problems. If losing weight solves even some of these problems, and if we can find an acceptable and effective way to lose weight, we really should go for it.

THE BENEFITS OF WEIGHT LOSS

CHAPTER 2

KEY POINTS

1 Weight loss is the most powerful therapy we have in medicine today.

2 Weight loss from the LAP-BAND™ System leads to the resolution of most of the diseases that arise from obesity.

3 Weight loss from the LAP-BAND™ System improves quality of life.

4 Substantial weight loss after placement of the LAP-BAND™ results in a marked improvement in length of life.

THE POWER OF WEIGHT LOSS

Weight loss is the most powerful therapy we have available in medicine today.

There is no other treatment that can make such a difference to so many health problems. There is no other therapy that improves people's quality of life so much. And, in particular, there is no other therapy that so clearly protects people from dying prematurely.

Chapter 1 highlighted the fact that many diseases are caused by or made worse by obesity. We have seen that obesity reduces the quality of people's lives by limiting them both physically and socially. Also, obesity is rapidly becoming the greatest cause of preventable death, even above smoking. It is natural to assume that, with weight loss, all these problems will go away, that everything will go back to normal and there will be no more trouble. This is not a reasonable assumption to make without some proof.

For instance, obesity could have already resulted in the damage having been done. Although the weight loss might slow the progression of disease, can it really reverse a disease process or improve quality of life after 20 or 30 years of disease? Even with weight loss, people may die just as prematurely, the patient with diabetes may continue to need insulin and the chronically unemployed may still not be able to get work. We need data. If we do not measure it we cannot know. Fortunately, we have now measured most of the problems of obesity and the results are reassuring.

ILLNESSES ASSOCIATED WITH OBESITY

Let's look at the illnesses associated with obesity first. Outlined below in boxes are some studies that we have done at the Centre for Obesity Research and Education at Monash University over the last 10 years. All of these studies have been published in the medical literature and are available from a medical library. If you want more detail than these brief summaries provide, please go to the sources and study the reports in more detail.

TYPE 2 DIABETES

Type 2 diabetes is the paradigm of an obesity-related disease. In most cases, it exists because of the obesity and, in most cases, it will disappear with weight loss. It is common, it generates multiple serious complications, and it is lethal.

Most people with type 2 diabetes are overweight and about half are obese. This is particularly well illustrated by the Nurses Cohort Study, an important ongoing study in the US, in which approximately 100,000 nurses have been followed for many years.4 Based on the risk of developing type 2 diabetes when the BMI is 21, this study showed that the risk of developing type 2 diabetes was five times greater at a BMI of 25, 35 times greater at a BMI of 30, and 93 times greater at or above a BMI of 35. It is estimated that there are now more than 20 million people with type 2 diabetes in the US and over one million in Australia. Given the morbidity and mortality that diabetes causes in young and middle-aged adults, this disease alone should elicit a very loud call for action against the rising epidemic of obesity.

Most of our patients who were diabetic before LAP-BAND™ placement have either become non-diabetic or have had a significant reduction in the medication they need to control their sugar levels.

STUDY BOX

We studied 60 patients who had diabetes and obesity with a BMI of 30–40. We randomly allocated them into a program of best care for their diabetes plus the gastric band (the test group) or just a program of best care for diabetes (the control group). At 2 years, three-quarters of those who had the band were free of any signs of diabetes and had stopped all treatment. They had also lost 70% of their excess weight. Almost all of the control group were still obese and still had their diabetes.[5]

No treatment other than weight loss can have such a powerful effect on diabetes. Most treatments strive just to limit the severity and dangers of the disease by keeping the blood sugar levels as near to normal as possible. Weight loss can take the disease away completely. Diabetes is a dreadful disease. It damages most systems of the body and severely shortens life expectancy. Weight loss can change the disease dramatically. If you are obese and have type 2 diabetes, it is essential that you lose weight. This should be seen as the most important part of the treatment of diabetes. If the simpler options of lifestyle change through less eating and more exercise have not succeeded, LAP-BAND™ placement must be considered.

HYPERTENSION

High blood pressure or hypertension is a major risk factor for heart attacks and strokes. It is much more common in the obese.

STUDY BOX

We followed 88 people with high blood pressure for 12 months after LAP-BAND™ placement and found that, by that time, 60% had returned to normal blood pressure and were off all treatment. Another 33% had found their blood pressure was much easier to control.[6]

ABNORMAL FATS IN THE BLOOD

Medically we call this problem dyslipidemia—"dys" means disordered, "lipid" is another word for fat and "emia" refers to the blood. In obese people the triglyceride levels are often elevated and the high-density lipoprotein (HDL) cholesterol, which is sometimes referred to as the "good" cholesterol, is abnormally low.

STUDY BOX

We followed several hundred patients for 4 years after LAP-BAND™ placement and found that the triglyceride and HDL cholesterol levels rapidly returned to normal and stayed there for at least the 4 years. As abnormality of these lipid levels is a clear risk factor for heart disease, this reduction in levels is regarded as very beneficial.[6]

REFLUX ESOPHAGITIS

Reflux esophagitis sometimes referred to as GERD, an abbreviation of gastroesophageal reflux disease. It is very common in the obese. More than half the people we see with severe obesity have some heartburn. This is the pain or uncomfortable feeling you get behind the breastbone when acid from the stomach travels up into the esophagus and irritates the lining enough to produce symptoms. About one in five of our patients will have this problem severely enough to have to take drug therapy to reduce the acid. If the disease continues for long enough, a change, known as Barrett's esophagus, can occur in the lining of the esophagus. This new lining is regarded as premalignant. It carries a 50 times increase in the chance of developing cancer of the esophagus.

Of the more than half of our patients who have heart-burn before the LAP-BAND™ placement, almost all are cured by the procedure.

STUDY BOX

We followed 88 patients who had a moderate or severe stage of GERD. At 12 months 90% had no further symptoms and were not taking any medication for the problem.[6]

The LAP-BAND™ is very good at blocking reflux. This is a direct effect of the band sitting at the very top of the stomach, where it can stop the acid moving up into the esophagus. The benefit is felt from immediately after operation, before any weight loss. We have had a lot of experience with the operation of Nissen fundoplication. This is a laparoscopic operation that is very good for controlling GERD in the general population. Our results with LAP-BAND™ placement are just as good as our results with Nissen fundoplication. For someone who has severe GERD and severe obesity, two problems are solved for the price of one.

SLEEP-DISORDERED BREATHING

The most significant disorder of breathing while asleep is obstructive sleep apnea and we will look at this problem below. Other breathing problems include habitual snoring, daytime sleepiness and poor sleep quality.

STUDY BOX

We looked at 313 of our obese patients before LAP-BAND™ placement and found that 59% of the men and 45% of the women had some form of disturbed sleep. We restudied 123 of these people at 1 year after band placement, by which time they had lost nearly half of their excess weight. Habitual snoring had decreased from 82% to 14% of patients, abnormal daytime sleepiness was reduced from 40% to 4% of patients, and poor sleep quality was reduced from 40% to 2% of patients. As a group they were snoring less, sleeping better and felt less tired during the day.[6]

We were a little surprised to find that the problems were nearly as common in the women as the men, even though men are much more likely to attract medical attention and have proper sleep assessments performed.

OBSTRUCTIVE SLEEP APNEA

Obstructive sleep apnea is a disease in which you stop breathing during your sleep. The word "apnea" means "no breathing." Typically, you are snoring away as usual and then there is a period of quiet. Your partner is delighted for the moment of peace and quiet, but anxious that there is absolutely no sound. You could be dead. There may be silence for up to a minute. Then, with a lot of grunts and snorts, you get going again back to heavy snoring.

What has happened is that the tissue in the neck has become too bulky and there is inadequate space. As you start to go into the deep phase of sleep, your muscles relax, and your tongue falls back and closes the small space present, blocking your airway. As the oxygen levels in the body fall, the brain stirs, wakes you up and tells you to get back to some serious breathing. You wake up, get some tone back in the tongue, the airway opens and the snoring show is back on the road. These episodes may happen 100 times a night. They are not good for the brain or the heart—or the marriage. You don't get a good night's sleep and are drowsy through the day. The drowsy driver is now recognized as a major contributor to road deaths. It is bad for you and dangerous for others.

In the study of sleep-disordered breathing described above, we found that one-third of the patients had observed sleep apnea before LAP-BAND™ placement. By that, we mean that their partner observed them stopping breathing during periods of heavy snoring. After weight loss, only 2% had the problem.

STUDY BOX

In a later study we examined sleep apnea more closely by doing sleep studies before and an average of 18 months after LAP-BAND™ placement. In the sleep study, each person has their sleep status and their breathing monitored overnight in a sleep laboratory. We studied 25 men and women who were massively obese with an average BMI of 53. Before operation, 23 had been diagnosed as having sleep apnea and were using continuous positive airway pressure (CPAP) machines to help them through the night. The other two had sleep apnea but were not using CPAP. After an average weight loss of 99 lb (45 kg) each, only six were still using their CPAP machines and all of those machines were set at lower pressures. As a group they also noticed a major improvement in other health measures — improved quality of life, less depression and less daytime sleepiness. The health benefits of weight loss for these people were very clear. And the pleasure of being able to go to bed at night without the mask and the machine was very gratefully received.[6]

ASTHMA

Asthma has only recently been recognized as an illness importantly associated with obesity. It is at least twice as common in obese children and adults as those with normal weight. Weight loss as a result of LAP-BAND™ placement has helped almost every one of our asthmatic patients. All find it easier to manage their asthma and to avoid severe attacks, and some have no more trouble with asthma after they have lost weight. In our studies we found a remarkable reduction in the need to be admitted to hospital for asthma. All patients who have asthma will show an improvement in association with weight loss after band placement.

In some cases, there will be no further attacks and no need for continuing therapy.

STUDY BOX

In a study of the specific effects of weight loss on asthma, we followed 33 patients for 1 year. All showed improvement, with fewer attacks and easier control. One-third of the patients had no asthma attacks at all during the year. In the year before the LAP-BAND™ procedure, nine of the group had had to be admitted to hospital on one or more occasions because of acute episodes of asthma. No admissions to hospital were needed in the year after operation.[6]

NON-ALCOHOLIC STEATOHEPATITIS (NASH)

This name is a bit of a mouthful but simply means inflammation of the liver ("hepatitis") associated with fat ("steato") and not due to excess alcohol consumption. The acronym NASH is easier to use. NASH occurs particularly in obese people who have a lot of their weight in the middle—the apple-shaped—and who are at risk of diabetes or already have diabetes. You may not have heard much about it but it is becoming recognized as a major health problem and is now one of the common diseases leading to the need for a liver transplant. If we think you are at risk of NASH, we will take a biopsy of the liver at the time of LAP-BAND™ placement to check for it.

STUDY BOX

We studied 36 patients who had a liver biopsy at the time of LAP-BAND™ placement and a second liver biopsy at approximately 2 years after band placement to check if the problem was resolving with weight loss. NASH was present at the initial biopsy in 23 of these patients but was present in only four of these people at repeat biopsy. The changes associated with weight loss had led to resolution of this dangerous condition in 19 of the 23 people.[6]

INFERTILITY AND POLYCYSTIC OVARY SYNDROME

Obesity leads to infertility in women, most commonly due to irregular ovulation or no ovulation at all. One particular condition that is common in obese women is polycystic ovary syndrome, often abbreviated to PCOS. In this condition there are abnormalities that lead to an excess of the male hormone, testosterone, in the circulation. Many of these women notice acne and excess hair on the face along with very irregular periods. Weight loss leads to correction of the hormonal problems, so that periods become more regular and fertility increases.

STUDY BOX

In a study of the hormonal changes in 107 obese women, 12 were shown to have PCOS initially. This resolved in 11 of the 12 as they lost weight.[6]

PREGNANCY

Not only are women more likely to become pregnant after losing weight, they will also have a better outcome. Pregnancy in severely obese women is associated with important risks to both the mother and the baby. Do women who have lost weight after LAP-BAND™ placement have fewer problems?

STUDY BOX

Our patients have had over 200 pregnancies after LAP-BAND™ placement. We compared these pregnancy outcomes with those of the pregnancies they had before band placement, and with the outcomes of pregnancy that we have come to expect in the general community.

After band placement the pregnant women did just fine. The weight gained during the pregnancy was about the right amount, 16–19 lb (7–9 kg). This was because of a very important asset of the LAP-BAND™—its adjustability. We can remove fluid if the weight gain is not ideal and allow a greater food intake, enough for the pregnant mother and the growing baby. Other bariatric procedures do not allow this margin of nutritional safety.

The birth weights of the babies were identical to those in the general community—about 7 lb (3.3 kg)—and there was about the same incidence of problems such as high blood pressure, diabetes and need for cesarean section as seen in the general community. These outcomes were clearly better than those for the previous pregnancies of these women before they had lost the weight.[7]

DEPRESSION

Depression is common in obese people.

> STUDY BOX
>
> We followed the outcome of 262 consecutive patients with LAP-BAND™ placement. We measured their level of depression before operation and found that they were almost equally divided into four groups. Approximately one-quarter were not depressed at all, and one-quarter each had mild depression, moderate depression or severe depression. We followed them for up to 4 years and noticed a major and durable improvement. At the end of the study three out of four were judged to be not depressed and very few were left with moderate or severe depression.[6]

THE BENEFITS OF WEIGHT LOSS

THE EFFECTS OF WEIGHT LOSS ON SURVIVAL

We all want to live a long life. We don't want to die prematurely. It is clear that obesity is associated with a reduced life expectancy due to the effects of all the diseases it causes. Heart disease, stroke, cancers and all the complications of diabetes are just some of the dangerous problems that could lead to early death. But do you live longer if you have been obese and lose weight?

STUDY BOX

We have been seeking the answer to this question by looking at the outcomes for our patients who have lost weight after LAP-BAND™ placement and comparing the number of deaths in our patients with an equivalent group of people who were obese but have not lost weight. In summary, we followed 961 patients for an average of 3.6 years and compared them to a group of 2119 obese patients who remained obese and who were followed for an average of 12 years. There have been no deaths in our patients from the band placement itself but four patients have died from causes such as heart attack and cancer in the years after surgery. A total of 225 have died in the group who have not lost weight. Once we adjust for the different length of follow-up and differences in age, sex and weight, the risk of dying has been reduced in the LAP-BAND™ group by 72%. The obese group had four times the risk of dying during the follow-up period compared to the group who lost weight after band placement.[8]

This is a very powerful effect. Hopefully it will cause the healthcare providers and administrators to take notice of the potential benefits of the LAP-BAND™ System and be more enthusiastic about funding the procedure. We often hear in the press about another "breakthrough" in medicine when a new treatment is able to achieve a 20% improvement in survival over the existing treatment. In this case there is a 400% increase, making LAP-BAND™ placement 20 times more powerful than some of the other breakthroughs noted in medicine.

QUALITY OF LIFE

Obesity has a major impact on the physical, psycho-social and economic health of patients and thus we could expect that it reduces quality of life. But how can we know? How can we measure quality of life? Fortunately, there are now quite a number of ways of doing this which are easy to do and have been shown to be valid measures. The most broadly accepted is a set of 36 questions known as the Medical Short Form (36) Health Survey or, more briefly, the SF-36. This questionnaire can measure quality of life across a range of health conditions.

> STUDY BOX
>
> We have used the SF-36 to assess quality of life in obese people and the changes to it along with weight loss after LAP-BAND™ placement. In one study we tested 459 patients before operation and then annually for 4 years. In the obese people all measures of the SF-36 were significantly lower than in the general community, indicating a markedly reduced quality of life. The values were equivalent to the reduced quality of life that can be measured in people with extensive cancer, crippling arthritis or stroke. At the end of the first year after band placement, all measures had returned to values that are normal for the community as a whole and they remained so for the 4 years of the study.[6]

However, perhaps the best demonstration of improvement in quality of life comes not from the dry science of our research but from the stories our patients tell us about the simple pleasures they recognize after weight loss:

1 being able to cross your legs when sitting
2 spending all day in the garden without having to stop every 15 minutes
3 not being the fattest person in the room
4 buying clothes off the rack
5 not having to take several prescription drugs every day
6 being confident enough to apply for a job and look forward to the interview
7 not being scared of trying on clothes when the label says "one size fits all"
8 going into good clothing shops and being offered assistance instead of being ignored
9 being able to buy a pair of jeans
10 having more self-confidence
11 going out to dinner and ordering an appetizer only, knowing that it will be more than enough
12 looking forward to going to a party
13 being able to get in and out of a car easily
14 climbing a flight of stairs without getting winded
15 having acquaintances say to you, "I heard you speak and knew it was your voice but I didn't recognize you"
16 getting outside and involved in the kids' activities
17 having your husband say how good you look, and, when he looks at photos of the "old" you, saying that he can't remember you looking the way you did
18 forgetting you have not eaten
19 no longer dreading the school reunion
20 not thinking about food
21 having the odd food treat and not feeling guilty
22 being able to walk for hours without chafing
23 being able to do up the seat belt on an airplane without the embarrassment of having to ask for an extension

24 feeling energized

25 enjoying moving—springing out of a chair instead of levering yourself out

26 playing sport again

27 keeping up with people walking, especially my husband who takes big strides

28 sitting on the floor, cross-legged

29 dancing; no longer being the fat one in the corner

30 getting down on the floor to play with the kids

31 knowing that my health has improved and that my life has been extended.

SUMMARY

These studies are provided to give you a summary of the remarkable health benefits for our patients after LAP-BAND™ placement. These results have all been published or are about to be published in the medical literature after careful scrutiny by experts. As a part of our commitment to keep in touch, we track our patients very carefully and are especially interested in the health benefits that are achieved. Substantial weight loss, as occurs after LAP-BAND™ placement, is the most powerful therapy we have in health care today. There is no drug or operation or other treatment that is close to the effectiveness of weight loss on a person with the disease of obesity and its associated illnesses. To have a gentle, safe and reliable way of achieving this weight loss, through LAP-BAND™ placement, is a great joy to us and a great benefit to our patients.

CHAPTER 3

THE OPTIONS FOR ACHIEVING WEIGHT LOSS

KEY POINTS

1 We must continue to seek preventive measures against obesity. Effective preventive measures are not yet available.

2 General expectations about what to achieve and what to avoid should be established before looking at the different options for weight loss.

3 Always begin with the simple and safe weight-loss procedures, and then move to the more complex and risky.

4 Non-surgical options are not yet effective enough for treating obesity.

5 The surgical options are all effective but vary in risk and changes to anatomy.

WAYS TO ACHIEVE WEIGHT LOSS

We have seen that obesity is a major problem and that weight loss is the most powerful therapy we have in health care today. It is now time to look at the options available for achieving this weight loss.

PREVENTION

Firstly, we must mention prevention. This has to be the most important aim.

With a problem so common, there is no way that we can ever treat all those who are or will become obese. We must try to prevent the problem arising in the first place. This has to be our first commitment, particularly to our children and adolescents.

We talk about primary prevention and secondary prevention. By primary prevention we mean avoiding obesity ever occurring. By secondary prevention, we mean preventing the diseases that can arise from obesity, even if we have not been able to prevent obesity itself.

Unfortunately, we are not yet very good at primary prevention. We have no successful programs that can be applied across our community to prevent the problem of obesity. We have a lot of good ideas, and plenty of theories and hypotheses. We even have some pilot studies that may show promise. But, to date, we have no proven, predictable way of prevention that is acceptable to the community and effective in preventing weight gain.

This is not all that surprising. We live in a culture that promotes eating and physical inactivity, reinforced by powerful commercial forces. To address this established culture will take a strong political will and a multidisciplinary approach. This address has not yet happened. We need to continue to look for good pathways to prevention, as they are not yet visible. Not only is the problem of obesity still a problem, it is in fact a worsening one. The numbers are increasing. We are losing ground. We are failing to prevent the problem. We have not yet even started to overcome the challenge.

We are a little better at secondary prevention. If you develop type 2 diabetes, we can help you control your blood sugar levels and so prevent some of the complications of the disease. If your blood pressure is too high or the fat levels in your blood are too high, we can give you medicine to control these problems and thereby reduce the chance of stroke or heart attack. However, this is a compromise. You still have the disease and the medicine is just reducing some of its harmful effects without taking it away or curing it. It would be far better to get rid of the disease altogether. With significant and durable weight loss, type 2 diabetes can go away, blood pressure can return to normal levels and the fat levels in the blood can return to normal. Most of the obesity-related diseases are either cured or markedly improved with weight loss. Naturally this is our preferred approach, so let us look at methods for achieving weight loss. In doing so, it should become clear why the LAP-BAND™ is our preferred option for those who have failed the simpler methods.

ACHIEVABLE EXPECTATIONS

Before looking at each of the options for reducing weight we should establish some general expectations of what we want to achieve and at what cost. We can then look at each option and measure its effect against these expectations.

WHAT SHOULD BE REQUIRED OF ALL TREATMENT OPTIONS?

1 Safety

Beyond all else we must try to avoid hurting people. Everything has possible side effects and complications. These need to be minimal. The method you select to lose weight is a choice you make. It is made on the balance between the good—the effectiveness—and the bad—the risks and the costs. The good should always far exceed the bad.

2 Effectiveness

The treatment option should be effective in achieving sufficient weight loss to solve your problem. If you are overweight, a small weight loss might suffice. If you are obese (BMI >30), you are more likely to need a substantial weight loss to solve your problems. Depending on your initial weight and BMI, a loss of 45–260 lb (20–120 kg) might be needed. Certainly, 11–22 lb (5–10 kg) is not going to be enough. You should also check that the treatment option offers good evidence of health benefits and a better quality of life along with weight loss.

3 Durability

Short-term weight loss has no particular value. In fact, it may even be harmful. Losing weight, even quite substantial amounts of weight, is not so hard. Most of our patients have done it many times before they come to see us. The real challenge is to keep that weight off for a long time. So we should look not only at the amount of weight loss a treatment can achieve but also for evidence that the weight loss lasts.

4 Minimal side effects

Being obese is unpleasant but you don't want to swap one type of unpleasantness for another. If a treatment creates its own problems, such as the oily rectal incontinence that results from taking orlistat or the smelly diarrhea from biliopancreatic diversion, it is not much fun. Check beforehand about the possible side effects of each treatment.

5 Controllability/adjustability

Lifestyle methods are controllable or adjustable, as you can control the amount you eat or the exercise you do. There is also some flexibility with the doses of drugs used for weight loss. For all surgical procedures, except the LAP-BAND™, you do not have this ability. In the future there will be more options that are adjustable but these are not yet available. Once the surgeon has left the operating room after a gastric bypass, there is nothing that can be done to vary the restriction created. If it's too tight, bad luck. If it's too loose, too bad. If it's just right, it may slowly alter over time and you or your physician cannot take it back to where it was without difficult surgery.

Having control is very important. Good weight-loss programs center on a partnership between you and your physician or other health professional. You both need to be able to exercise some control of the treatment to optimize the effect. Without doubt, the adjustability of the LAP-BAND™ is its greatest single asset—it allows you to control your level of satiety.

6 Reversibility

We can easily stop a diet or a course of drug treatment. We can remove an intragastric balloon. However, the LAP-BAND™ is the only surgical procedure that is easily reversible. Reversibility is almost as important as adjustability, for two reasons. Firstly, we are all skeptical. We worry that something promised may not turn out just so. You do not want to be trapped into something that may not turn out to be what you expected. With the LAP-BAND™, you are not trapped in a permanent state. It can be removed easily and everything goes back to normal. However, this is not so with other surgical pro-cedures—they are there for life.

The second reason to prefer reversibility is that we can only look so far into the future. At the moment there is nothing better than the LAP-BAND™ in view. However, in 20 years, and maybe even in 15 years, a dramatically better treatment may be discovered. You don't want to be locked into something that is well past its use-by date. You want to be able to choose the best current option.

If, however, in the meantime, you have gone ahead with the LAP-BAND™, you can at least be comforted that, if some magical new therapy does arise which works superbly and has minimal side effects, you can have the band removed as a day procedure, the stomach will return to normal and you can start on the new "magical" treatment. The LAP-BAND™ is fully reversible.

Not so if you have had a gastric bypass. This is a very difficult procedure to reverse as the stomach has been divided completely and the intestines have been dramatically rearranged. As for a sleeve gastrectomy, most of the stomach has been removed. It is gone. For these patients, there can be no going back.

7 Low reoperation/revision rate

Naturally, you would like to have one procedure and that will be that. Unfortunately, this does not always happen. Something may change or leak or block or break, and thus may lead to the need for additional procedures. Each of the surgical procedures has a maintenance requirement. You need to be aware how likely reoperation is and how complex and risky is the revision.

8 Minimal invasiveness

If you are going to have surgery, you will want to have as little trauma and change to your gut as possible. Look for the procedure that interferes with the tissue of the gut the least. Ask about what is done for each procedure. Are organs or parts of them removed? Are segments of the gut closed off or redirected? Is there joining of one part of the gut to another? Remember, leaking from these joins is the major cause of death in patients who undergo surgery. Gastric banding is essentially always laparoscopic. It is gentle. It requires very little dissection. It is often performed as an outpatient procedure. There is a world of difference between the minimal invasiveness of the band and the invasiveness of the alternative procedures.

THE TREATMENT OPTIONS

We will now review the options available. The first step in solving your problem with obesity is to commit to losing weight. Lock onto that commitment. Accept that your problem is too severe and too dangerous to continue with. Committing to lose a substantial amount of weight must come before seeking the solution. The second step is to determine how to achieve weight loss. From the range of treatment options, you should start with the simplest and safest before moving on to the more complex and risky. If you are truly committed to losing weight, somewhere along that series you will find the correct option for you. It does require true commitment. You cannot just go part of the way and then give up. You must stay committed.

The list of desirable features above should help you find the right option. We will return to this list after we have looked at the strengths and the weaknesses of each of the different treatment options. Keep this list of features in mind as we look at what each of the treatment options has to offer. See Table 4.1 on page 78 for a list of how well each treatment option fulfills the ideal.

1 LIFESTYLE

The lifestyle solution is to eat less food and have plenty of activity. This solution is simple to prescribe yet it is very difficult to achieve sustainable outcomes with it.

Across the world and across generations a healthy life-style through good eating and exercise practices has been constantly promoted; yet the problem of obesity is not just continuing but increasing.

Almost everyone can lose some weight by a diet or exercise program. The challenge is to lose enough weight to make a difference and, more importantly, to keep it off. Weight loss for 1 or 2 years is not much help to your health. You need to lose weight permanently. Very few will lose weight by lifestyle change alone and be able to keep that weight off for even 5 years.

The commercial weight-loss centers have made for-tunes by promising excellent weight loss through various twists on the "lifestyle" methods, and their advertise-ments always show the classic "before and after" pictures. Invariably, the "after" picture is only months after. They do not show the "5 years after" pictures.

A recent comprehensive review of all the high-quality scientific studies of the options for weight control has found that there is no evidence of a durable effect from any current lifestyle intervention methods for obesity.[9] We would hope that lifestyle approaches could at least prevent the problem. This prevention has not yet been achieved. Rather, the problem of obesity is increasing. If we are failing to prevent it, we must have less hope of curing it once it is established. The results are there-fore not surprising.

Very-low-calorie diet

One particular form of dietary therapy that can have a powerful effect in the short term is the very-low-calorie diet (VLCD). The best-known form of the VLCD is called Optifast™. This involves taking three sachets of a specially formulated powder each day and almost no other food. Each sachet is made up into a liquid meal with water. You are allowed a small amount of vegetables at night as the only additional intake. If you follow the rules completely you will be receiving between 500 and 600 calories (2100 and 2520 kJ) per day and we would expect you to lose 22–44 lb (10–20 kg) over a 3-month period. It is not recommended that you continue beyond 3 months and it is uncommon to succeed so well with a second course later on.

However, you can get good weight loss in the short term. The VLCD provides perhaps our best method for achieving a significant weight loss quickly without resorting to weight-loss surgery. There can be reasons why this is a good idea. A common one is as a preparation for a surgical procedure such as a knee or hip operation. We frequently use the VLCD in some patients as a preparation for the LAP-BAND™ procedure, particularly if they have severe central obesity. As it is not continued permanently, you cannot expect to achieve a medium- or long-term weight loss with the VLCD.

2 DRUG THERAPY

We do not yet have drugs that are truly effective for treating obesity. Until recently two drugs were available for long-term use for achieving and maintaining weight loss—orlistat (sold as Xenical™) and sibutramine (sold as Meridia™ or Reductil™). Both are able to help treat people who are overweight but neither has proven to be sufficiently powerful to be reliable for treating people with obesity. Their long-term efficacy is poor and long-term safety unknown. A review of all the clinical trials of these drugs shows that the average weight loss after 1 year of orlistat is about 7 lb (3 kg) and for sibutramine is 10 lb (4.5 kg).[10] For those with obesity, who must lose 50 lb (23 kg) or more, these results are just not good enough. Sibutramine has now been withdrawn from the market because of side effects on the heart. No new drugs have been sufficiently safe and effective to be approved in the last 12 years.

Most of our patients have tried some of the drug therapies before considering the LAP-BAND™. Anything may be worth a try if the problems of obesity can be overcome. However, it is best not to expect too much—they are simply not that good. Furthermore, they are usually expensive, they may have unpleasant or even serious side effects, and the thought of taking one of these drugs every day for years and years in order to get a few pounds of weight off is just not acceptable to most people, especially when so little weight loss is achieved.

We definitely need better drugs for obesity. No doubt they will come. We may one day find a pill that truly takes away your appetite, or increases the wasting of energy. There may be some gene therapy that makes you thin forever. The pharmaceutical companies are working very hard to find such drugs or treatments. Given that there is nothing that is dramatically good on the horizon and that drugs take 5–10 years from development to market, we probably should not anticipate success from drug therapy in the next 15 years and possibly not in the next 20 years.

3 ENDOSCOPIC PROCEDURES

Endoscopic procedures are those whereby a gastroscope, which is a long flexible tube of light fibers, optical fibers and other channels, is passed through the mouth, down the esophagus and into the stomach. These procedures have not yet established a role in the treatment of obesity, but there is plenty of effort going into seeking an effective method.

Intragastric balloons are the only endoscopic method that is currently in clinical practice around the world. With this method, an empty balloon is passed through the mouth into the stomach. It is then filled with about a pint (0.5 L) of saline and thereby creates a large mass in the stomach. The idea is that you feel full and do not eat so much. After 6 months, the balloon must be removed as it may rupture and cause a blockage further down the gut.

The intragastric balloons had a period of enthusiastic usage in the 1980s until carefully performed clinical trials showed them to be ineffective. A new version of the intragastric balloon, the BioEnterics Intragastric Balloon™, commonly known as the BIB™, has been developed with the proposal that it overcomes all the weaknesses of the earlier balloons. It is being used in Europe, Mexico and South America. It is approved for clinical use in Australia but not yet in the US.

In the clinical reports available the BIB™ appears to work, but high-quality clinical trials have yet to demonstrate its effectiveness. It can be left in place for only 6 months, during which time there may be a weight loss of 35 lb (16 kg) or more. The lost weight is likely to return after its removal. Nevertheless, it does appear to make a difference, it does not involve an operation and it is reversible.

There is a high level of research activity toward finding other methods of achieving weight loss that involve endoscopic techniques. These include ways of suturing or stapling the stomach through the endoscope to simulate what is done in some surgical procedures. It is likely that some of these procedures will appear soon and be publicized as the ultimate solution. It is even more likely that their benefit will, in fact, be modest and short term. We just have to wait and see what happens.

4 WEIGHT-LOSS (BARIATRIC) SURGERY

The surgical treatment of obesity is called bariatric surgery after the Greek words, *baros*, meaning "weight," and *iatrikos*, meaning "the art of healing." It is the most rapidly growing area of surgical practice in the Western world today. This rapid growth is due to the ability of bariatric procedures to provide a solution to an otherwise insoluble problem and the evolution of safer, less invasive and more conservative forms of procedures.

The surgical treatment of obesity has evolved over a period of more than 50 years. Today there are four bariatric procedures in use: gastric bypass, biliopancreatic diversion, sleeve gastrectomy and laparoscopic adjustable gastric banding. Small bowel bypass is no longer performed.

Small bowel bypass

This procedure was introduced in the 1950s and there were various ways in which the operation was performed. Each method, however, shared the common principle of bypassing the normal absorptive capacity of the gut. In other words, you could eat quite a lot but the food wouldn't be absorbed into the body. Instead, you would have diarrhea. Such procedures were generally effective in achieving weight loss but they had a number of serious side effects, which ultimately has made them unacceptable.

Roux-en-Y gastric bypass

Roux-en-Y gastric bypass (RYGB) was introduced more than 35 years ago and is still commonly used. It does require major manipulation of the gut. About half of the operations are performed by the traditional open surgical approach with a long incision in the abdomen, and half are performed laparoscopically (by keyhole surgery).

The operation can be performed in a number of different ways but they all achieve their effect through two common features. Firstly, they create a small upper stomach so that you can only eat a small amount of food at any one time before you feel comfortably or uncomfortably full. Secondly, they each delay the emptying of the food from that small upper stomach into the rest of the gut in some way so that the feeling of fullness stays with you after the meal and you are not inclined to eat between meals.

In RYGB, a stapling device is used to cut and separate completely a small piece of the top of the stomach from the rest of the stomach. The top part becomes the new stomach and the rest is closed off and not accessible anymore. The upper part of the small intestine is then divided completely, again with the stapling device. One of the divided ends is attached to the new stomach to allow the food to enter the rest of the gut. The other end is joined to the small intestine further downstream so that the digestive juices from the liver, gallbladder, duodenum and pancreas can get back into the digestive pathway. Figure 3.1 shows the end result of these multiple changes.

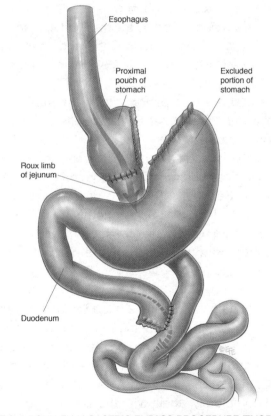

Esophagus

Proximal
pouch of
stomach

Excluded
portion of
stomach

Roux limb
of jejunum

Duodenum

FIGURE 3.1 ROUX-EN-Y GASTRIC BYPASS PROCEDURE (RYGB)

RYGB is a big operation with a real risk of major complications, and people die from these complications. It causes major changes in the gut and is essentially irreversible. It is a relatively complex procedure that provides no opportunity for adjustment after the operation.

Biliopancreatic diversion

Biliopancreatic diversion, commonly abbreviated to BPD, was introduced in the 1970s. This complex procedure removes much of the stomach and bypasses much of the gut. This procedure aims to reduce the size of the stomach to restrict intake, and also to prevent absorption of the food by diverting it from the digestive enzymes of the gut. Although it can be done laparoscopically, it is generally performed through an abdominal incision to reduce the risks. About half to three-quarters of the stomach is removed completely. The small intestine is then divided and reconnected in such a way that the food goes one way (the alimentary limb) and the digestive enzymes go another way (the biliopancreatic limb). Most of the enzymes are reabsorbed before they can do anything. The rest of the enzymes meet the food in the last 20 in (50 cm) of the small intestine—the common channel—to permit some limited absorption of food.

A variation of the BPD is known as the duodenal switch. It differs in only a minor way by changing the way most of the stomach is removed to retain the lower part of the stomach. It is not clear that there is any important difference between the two procedures.

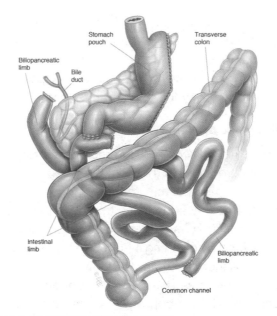

FIGURE 3.2 BILIOPANCREATIC DIVERSION

The BPD generally achieves good weight loss but at the cost of significant symptoms and a serious risk of malnutrition, and so is not performed often. It has the highest likelihood of death associated with the surgery of all the bariatric procedures.

Sleeve gastrectomy

This procedure started life as the first stage of the biliopancreatic diversion/duodenal switch (BPD-DS) operation, which we have just discussed. Then surgeons found that during the first year there was good weight loss with the sleeve component alone and they did not need to go on with the rest of the BPD-DS. Figure 3.3 shows what happens.

About 90% of the stomach is removed and the part that is left is shaped into a tube. You cannot eat as much and you lose weight, quite rapidly. In the first year, you will lose as much weight with the sleeve as

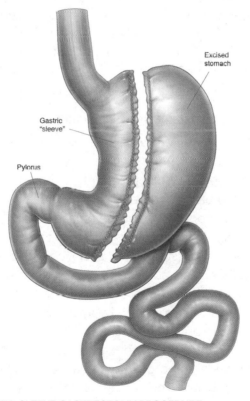

FIGURE 3.3 SLEEVE GASTRECTOMY PROCEDURE

you will lose with RYGB. But there is not usually much weight loss after that. On average people will lose about 55% of their excess weight. Think of your excess weight as the fat. You are losing about 55% of your fat, which is a good result if maintained.

There are two major concerns with sleeve gastrectomy. Firstly, it carries the risks of bypass for no better weight loss than the band. Secondly, as there is no reinforcement of the tube of stomach, it will inevitably expand and so, after a few years, you will be putting weight back on. Short-term weight loss, even for 4 to 5 years, is just not worth it.

Laparoscopic adjustable gastric banding

The LAP-BAND™ is an example of laparoscopic adjustable gastric banding and has been available since the 1990s. LAP-BAND™ placement is far more gentle and safe than the preceding operations. It is almost always done laparoscopically (by keyhole surgery) and it involves very little handling or dissection of tissue. Nothing is cut or stapled or removed or redirected. The band is placed across the very top of the stomach. There is almost no stomach above the band. With minimal dissection a pathway is made across the back of the top of the stomach, and the band is placed along that pathway, closed and fixed into that position by suturing some of the stomach wall across the front of the band. The tubing is then connected to

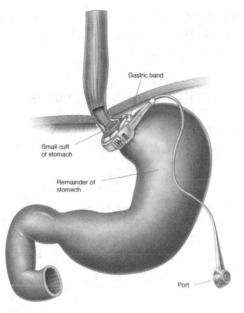

Gastric band

Small cuff
of stomach

Remainder of
stomach

Port

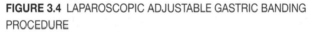

FIGURE 3.4 LAPAROSCOPIC ADJUSTABLE GASTRIC BANDING
PROCEDURE

an access port that is placed under the skin of the
abdominal wall.

The band compresses the wall of the stomach to cause
a feeling of satiety. There are special nerves there that
detect the pressure and send signals to the brain indicating that your stomach is full and that you don't need
any food. If the band is adjusted optimally, there is a
background sense of not being hungry that is present 24 hours a day. Then, as you eat, food is squeezed

across the band causing further compression of the nerves and sending extra bursts of signals to the brain, further reducing any sense of hunger.

WHICH PROCEDURE IS THE MOST COMMON?

There is significant variation in the preferred procedure between countries, often reflecting local regulatory and insurance factors.

In the US, gastric banding is now the most common option, just ahead of RYGB. The LAP-BAND™ did not become available in the US until 2001 and many insurance groups are still trying to avoid offering this option to their participants. However, the number of bands placed is increasing rapidly and it is expected to become the most popular option by far as the combination of safety, gentleness and effectiveness becomes well known.

In Australia, the LAP-BAND™ is the procedure of choice for more than 90% of people, with sleeve gastrectomy and RYGB making up most of the rest of the procedures.

Biliopancreatic diversion is now a very uncommon procedure everywhere because of the risks, the constant presence of an offensive diarrhea and concerns about the effects of a long-term lack of key nutrients. In many countries it is not used at all.

COMPARISON OF PROCEDURES

At their best, RYGB and the other stomach stapling procedures are very good. They enable a good weight loss without too many side effects. However, they are not at their best often enough. The real dilemma with stomach stapling is how to create a new stomach that is exactly right on the day of operation and which remains exactly right for the rest of the patient's life. This challenge is obviously too difficult. The body will always be changing, particularly stretching, in response to pressure. The lack of adjustability is a fatal flaw.

Sometimes the settings are too tight initially, resulting in severe vomiting. At other times the settings are too loose, leading to insufficient weight loss. Most commonly, the settings are about right at the time of operation, but change over subsequent months and years so that, with stretching or with breakdown of the staple line, there is a return toward a normal stomach and the weight-reducing effect is lost.

With sleeve gastrectomy or RYGB, the best weight loss is in the first year. Generally, if you have not lost enough weight by then, you are not going to lose any more. The weight starts to come back on again after the second or third year. Because there is no way to adjust the settings after the operation, there is no way to control the weight regain. It is very difficult for us to be sure about how durable the weight loss is after the gastric stapling procedures because more than half the people who have the operation are lost to follow-up by 5 years and so we cannot measure their weight. For those who are still being seen, it is most commonly reported that they have lost between 50% and 60% of their excess weight. If we assume that the ones who are missing have done less well—the usual reason why people stop coming to follow-up—the weight loss is probably well under 50% of excess weight at 10 years. This is not as good as the results that have been achieved with the LAP-BAND™.

STUDY BOX

We performed a very thorough analysis of the medical literature bringing together all the reports on RYGB and all the reports on LAP-BAND™ placement. We carefully analyzed the data from these reports and created a series of charts showing the reported weight loss for both procedures. Figure 3.5 shows the data. As can be seen, weight loss after a gastric bypass procedure is better than that after the LAP-BAND™ during the first 2 years. However, by the third year the differences are small and after that there are no differences to the 8-year point.[11]

Although stomach stapling is an acceptable option for some people, it has proved to be unacceptable to the vast majority of those in the community who are obese, either because of its risks and invasiveness or because of the difficulties in retaining the correct settings over

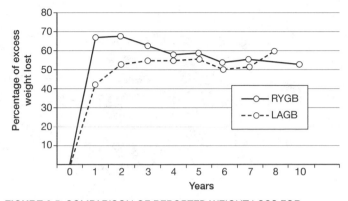

FIGURE 3.5 COMPARISON OF REPORTED WEIGHT LOSS FOR
ROUX-EN-Y GASTRIC BYPASS (RYGB) AND LAPAROSCOPIC
ADJUSTABLE GASTRIC BANDING (LAGB)

a long period. It can be estimated that only one of
every 200 people who have severe obesity in the US
would agree to a gastric bypass or other form of stomach stapling. The other 199 either have accepted their
problem of obesity or are looking for a more acceptable alternative.

The LAP-BAND™ procedure has been developed
to retain the good things that we have learned from
stomach stapling, but to overcome the problems that
made stomach stapling generally unacceptable. The
key features of the LAP-BAND™ that have led to its
wide acceptance are its safety, minimal invasiveness,
adjustability, reversibility and overall effectiveness. In
our practice, we used RYGB for many years before
the LAP-BAND™ became available; however, we have

not offered it as the first treatment of obesity since 1993, as it is clearly more dangerous, it is not adjustable or reversible, and it is no more effective in the medium term than the LAP-BAND™. We should always prefer the simple and safe over the complex and risky. We don't crack a nut with a sledgehammer if a nutcracker is available.

In Chapter 4, we look at how the gastric band works and we begin to look at how you must work with the band to get an optimal result. In Chapter 5, we look at all the good features of the LAP-BAND™ and discuss what expectations are reasonable with regard to weight loss. We will also look at the problems and unfavorable features of the LAP-BAND™. We will then describe the type of people who would be best treated with the LAP-BAND™. From this you will be able to determine whether this may be a suitable procedure for you.

HOW THE BAND WORKS AND HOW YOU WORK WITH THE BAND

CHAPTER 4

KEY POINTS

- The LAP-BAND™ AP is our preferred gastric band.

- The appetite centre of the brain tells us we should eat.

- The band sends signals to the appetite centre telling it to be quiet.

- A background of satiety occurs because the band squeezes steadily on the stomach.

- Each bite of food is squeezed across the band further reducing appetite.

WHICH BAND IS BEST?

There are a number of adjustable gastric bands available across the world. Some have come and gone, failed and disappeared. Others are new and untested. For most, we have almost no information regarding their safety or effectiveness and therefore they cannot be recommended. There are only two gastric bands for which a good amount of information is available about their safety and effectiveness, the LAP-BAND™ made by Allergan, a company based in Irvine, California, and the REALIZE™ band made by Ethicon Endosurgery, a part of the Johnson & Johnson Company, based in Cincinnati, Ohio. These two bands are the only ones that have been approved by the US Government for use in the US. I cannot see any good basis currently for considering any alternative bands. Of these two bands, I prefer the LAP-BAND™ and I have used it exclusively in all our gastric band procedures and in all of our research.

The LAP-BAND™ was the first laparoscopic adjustable gastric band available. I was involved in its original development in the early 1990s and in establishing its optimal use in clinical practice. It has now been in clinical use since 1993. We have learned a great deal since then and we have published a great deal. There have been more than 1,000 scientific reports on outcomes after the LAP-BAND™. As all of our experience and all of our research has been with the LAP-BAND™, the comments throughout the book relate to that particular band. For clarity and simplicity, however, I will sometimes use the generic term, gastric band, rather than the product name of LAP-BAND™. In this chapter I describe how far we have traveled in understanding how the LAP-BAND™ works. We are not able to confirm from our own experience or from the published literature whether other bands share most or all of these characteristics.

THE ANATOMY OF THE LAP-BAND™

Figure 4.1 shows a photo of the LAP-BAND™ AP System. AP stands for Advanced Platform. This model was introduced in 2006. There are some technical advantages for the AP band but the safety and the effectiveness are very similar to the earlier versions of the LAP-BAND™. Therefore, if you have had a LAP-BAND™ placed before 2006, be assured it is still just fine and will be just as effective as the newer version.

The band consists of a ring of silicone with an inner balloon. The balloon is connected by tubing to an access port. The most important single element of the gastric band is the inflatable balloon on the inner aspect of the band. This allows for tightening or loosening of the band. You can see in the picture two levels of adjustment of the band. In the first, there is 3 mL of saline present and there is a relatively large space in

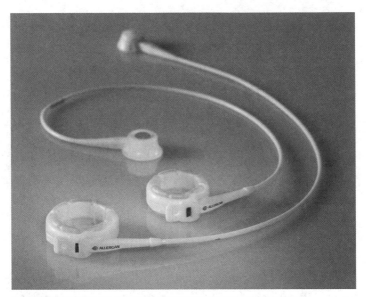

FIGURE 4.1 THE LAP-BAND™, SHOWING THE SILICONE RING
CONNECTED BY TUBING TO THE ACCESS PORT

the middle for the stomach to lie. In the second picture there is 8 mL of saline in the band and the space is smaller. Therefore the band would be squeezing much more tightly on the stomach.

The access port is most commonly placed about half-way between the bottom of the sternum (breastbone) and the umbilicus and about 1 in (2.5 cm) to the left of the midline. It is deep under the skin but in front of the muscle wall and is attached to a sheath of tough fibrous tissue that covers the muscle layer. If you are lying flat on a bunk, usually with a pillow placed under

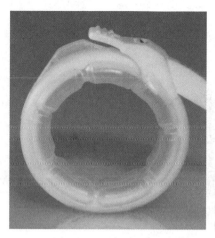

FIGURE 4.2 THE SILICONE RING OF THE LAP-BAND™ BEFORE THE INNER BALLOON IS INFLATED

the middle of your back to push your tummy forward, we can feel the access port and can push a needle through the skin and through the compressed silicone plug into the port. We now have access to the fluid in the system and can easily add or remove fluid to achieve the optimal level of adjustment of the band. By adding fluid, we reduce your appetite. By taking out fluid, we increase your appetite.

Figure 4.2 shows a close-up of the ring of silicone. The inner balloon is not inflated at all and is only just visible. Notice also the locking device.

In Figure 4.3, 8 mL of saline has been added to the inner balloon and you can see how the space has been reduced. This will narrow the opening from the upper stomach into the rest of the stomach, giving a greater

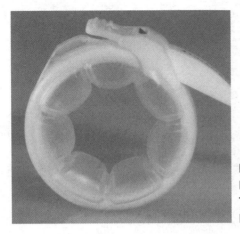

FIGURE 4.3 THE
LAP-BAND™ WITH
THE INNER BALLOON
PARTIALLY INFLATED

sense of satiety and making it more difficult to eat too much. By adjusting the amount of fluid in the balloon we can set the limits on your appetite and help you set limits on the volume of food intake.

Once the band is in place, it is like we now have a dial on your tummy. We can turn one way to make you more hungry or we can turn the other way to make you less hungry.

This is the magic of the gastric band. By placing the band, we can now easily control one of the most important drivers of eating—your hunger. The operation of placing the gastric band system is just setting the scene. The real value comes with the aftercare when we adjust the band to give you optimal control of your hunger.

Let us now look at the different components of your body that are involved with eating and how the band changes some of them.

THE BRAIN AND APPETITE

Our brain tells us to eat. The drive to eat comes from a special area deep in the brain, called the hypothalamus, and from a special area within the hypothalamus known as the arcuate nucleus. The arcuate nucleus is the coordinating center. It brings together signals from many different parts of the body.

The drive to eat has two components, called homeostatic eating and hedonic eating.

HOMEOSTATIC EATING

First and foremost, the brain tells us to eat because we need food. This is sometimes referred to as homeostatic eating, eating to stay alive. It maintains our state of health, it provides the energy and building blocks to repair and replace the bits that need maintenance and to grow new tissue. If you don't eat, you die. This is eating to live. The homeostatic drive to eat was a crucial drive when food was in short supply. The hunter–gatherer of the Stone Age could never be sure of an adequate supply of food. Strong signals were important to direct much of the daily activity of the Stone Age man and woman to hunting and gathering. Without these strong signals to focus them on maintaining nutrition, they could have starved. Today, we have the opposite situation. Today, we have too much food, too easily obtained—tasty, hygienic, available 24 hours a day and at relatively low cost. Today, this hunger drive is working against us as it leads to obesity with its associated risks of diseases and premature death. The signals to the hypothalamus encouraging homeostatic eating come from various parts of the body including the fat (adipose tissues), the stomach and other parts of the gut.

HEDONIC EATING

We also eat because we look forward to the pleasures of eating—the tastes, textures and flavors of food in the mouth, and the social activity and relaxation associated with eating. We eat because of the time of day. We have developed the habit of eating in the morning, at midday and in the evening. Even if we are not hungry, a voice tells us we should think about eating. This drive to eat is referred to as hedonic eating. The word "hedonism" is from the Greek and refers to the seeking of pleasure and avoidance of pain. This is sometimes contrasted with the homeostatic eating as living to eat rather than eating to live. The messages for hedonic eating come from within the brain itself. It sends signals to the hypothalamus to generate a feeling of hunger. It also stimulates an urge to eat without us being hungry, the "non-hunger" eating. We all do it. Who among us can see a table laden with delicious food and not try something that looks particularly appetizing? Even if we have just eaten and the thought of food is of no interest, we cannot resist having a taste, to enjoy that particular flavor or texture. Some do it more than others. Some use non-hunger eating as a comfort from stress or conflict or negative feelings. Non-hunger eating is a potent factor in generating obesity, not only because it is eating in excess of need but also because it is often spread through the day and is well described as "grazing."

The hypothalamus receives these various inputs and generates a sense of hunger. You become aware of a feeling of the need to eat, a wish to eat and an appetite to eat. Unless you are distracted by strong alternative signals, such as very active mental or physical activity, it increases to dominate your attention. It moves from being a mild sense of hunger, a gentle nudge toward having some food, to a stronger sense of hunger and eventually an almost painful state of extreme hunger.

SATIETY AND SATIATION

Once you have eaten, the drives to eat quieten down and a different group of signals commence. These can be described by the words "satiety" and "satiation." We use the term satiety to mean a sense of not being

TABLE 4.1 THE HUNGER/SATIETY SCALE

Hunger/ Satiety Scale	Description	Associated activity level	Ability to concentrate
1	**Uncomfortably full** Bloated; ashamed that you have gone so far over the top; making promises that you will never do it again.	**Very low** Not interested in moving much at all.	Very low
2	**Completely satisfied** You really do not want to eat another thing.	**Low** Would prefer to just sit and talk, or just sit.	Low
3	**Comfortable** Maybe could try something small and sweet—eating for pleasure not nutrition.	**Fair** Not too bad. Happy to go for a walk.	Fair
4	**Satisfied** No sense of hunger. Could eat more but do not need to.	**Good** Buzzing around getting things done.	Good
5	**Neutral** Not too interested in food, but would eat it if it was there. Typical halfway through a meal.	**Good** Buzzing around getting things done.	Very good
6	**Minimal hunger** Ready to eat but happy to defer for a while.	**Good** Buzzing around getting things done.	Very good
7	**Mild hunger** Starting to think about food, but can be distracted by important activity/interests.	**Good** Buzzing around, getting things done.	Good
8	**Moderate hunger** Not able to focus easily on anything else—looking for food as main task.	**Fair** A little distracted but able to get things done.	Fair
9	**Severe hunger** Cannot think of anything else but the need for food. Not able to work effectively.	**Low** Not interested in thinking about anything other than eating.	Poor
10	**Extreme hunger** Would eat (almost) anything just to get something into the stomach.	**Very low** Prefer to stay quiet. Only activity would be getting food.	Very poor

hungry. It is a feeling you should have for most of the day if you are eating regularly. It is at the other end of the spectrum from extreme hunger. Satiation is the feeling immediately after a meal of no longer being hungry, a feeling that the sense of hunger that was present before a meal is now under control. The two terms are very similar in meaning but, in discussing how the gastric band works, it is useful to separate them.

The gastric band generates both satiety and satiation. It works by sending a message from the stomach to the hypothalamus that there is no need to eat. It can be divided into two processes. Firstly, it generates a background sense of satiety, of not being hungry, that is present 24 hours a day. If the band is adjusted correctly, you should have an overall lowering of the hunger signal. A frequent comment from my patients is: "The best thing about the band is that I just do not feel hungry. For the first time in my life, I do not feel hungry."

This is the satiety signal at work.

Secondly, when you do eat, the sense of satiation comes quickly. Just a small amount of food will turn off whatever feeling of hunger there is. You will still get a little hungry after the band, but it is controlled with a small meal whereas previously a larger meal was needed.

The net result of the band generating a background of satiety and then the early onset of satiation after eating is less food eaten per day. Initially, it is less than the body needs and so you use up the stored energy from fat. You lose weight. Later, once you settle at a new steady level of weight, you are in balance. You are eating exactly the amount you need for homeostasis; you are eating correctly for the first time in your life. And this is a very small amount of food.

Table 4.1 provides a scale of hunger and satiety, graded from 1 to 10. We want you to always remain in the middle of that scale, between 4 (satisfied) and 7 (mild hunger). If you have eaten too much or too quickly, you will move to level 3. This is a risky area. Try to avoid it. Certainly never get to level 2. At the other end of the scale, with correct adjustment of the band, you should not become even moderately hungry. That would mean you are in the yellow zone. You need the band adjusted. If you are in the green zone, at most you should get just a little hungry. Then a small meal will take away that hunger, you move to level 5 or 4, and stop. Don't eat any more. Discard what is left and look forward to many hours before you need to think of food again.

We will return to the brain and how it receives signals from the stomach that generate satiety and satiation in a moment. Firstly, we need to understand what happens as you eat and how the band changes this.

CHEWING FOOD PROPERLY

Everyone's mother would have taught her children to chew their food properly. Chewing is the first step in breaking up food to allow its digestion. It has always been a good idea. After gastric banding, it becomes essential. After gastric banding, you must chew your food thoroughly. I do not want you to swallow any lumps of food. You must chew each bite of food until it is mush, until it has the consistency of mashed potato. Any piece of food that you anticipate cannot be reduced to mush should not be taken in. Red meat and fresh bread are two common examples of foods that are difficult to reduce to mush. They tend to stay in lumps. If you do put the wrong food in your mouth and find a lump that cannot be reduced to mush, you must spit it out. Do not swallow it.

Chewing well also provides an opportunity to enjoy the food more. We want you to enjoy eating as much or even more than before the band. However, focus on the quality of the food not the quantity. Eat the very best food. You can afford it. You are eating so little that the total cost will still be less. Chewing food well is a chance to savor its tastes. We so often eat without con-sciousness of the taste of the food. It has been swal-lowed before we have any awareness of its taste. If we were asked what the bite of food tasted like, we could not say. I want you to enjoy the tastes, the textures and

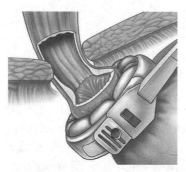

FIGURE 4.4 THE LAP-BAND™ SITS AT THE VERY TOP OF THE STOMACH, JUST BELOW THE END OF THE ESOPHAGUS

the flavors of your food. Think about them and improve your eating enjoyment.

The size of the bite is important. It must be small. We would like you to eat with a small fork or spoon. An oyster fork is a good example of a suitable size. A cake fork also is about the right size, but I would rather you not choose it for fear you might be tempted to put it to its rightful use.

SQUEEZING EACH BITE ACROSS THE BAND

The esophagus is a muscular tube, about 10 in (25 cm) long, which takes the food from the back of the mouth and delivers it into the stomach. It is quite powerful and squeezes the food along by a process of sequential contractions known as peristalsis. It will generate pressures that are about equivalent to a firm handshake. When

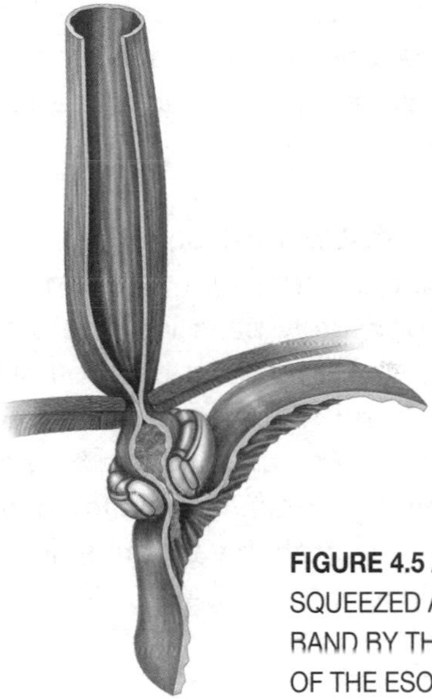

FIGURE 4.5 A SMALL BITE OF FOOD BEING SQUEEZED ACROSS THE AREA OF THE BAND BY THE STRONG CONTRACTIONS OF THE ESOPHAGUS

there is no band present, the bottom end of the esophagus opens up as the bite of food arrives and lets it pass into the stomach without any delay. The presence of the band makes a critical change to this process.

Examine Figures 4.4 and 4.5 closely. It is very important. Note the esophagus above, a small cuff of stomach and then the band. I want every bite of food to have crossed completely through the band before you swallow another bite. The band makes a narrow segment at the very top of the stomach. So, when the bite of food arrives there the esophagus has to squeeze the bite of food across the band for it to enter the main part of the stomach. A single bite of food that has been reduced to mush in the mouth will require several squeezes to move it fully past the band.

This squeezing takes time. Up to 6 squeezes might be necessary, in which case it would take up to a minute for the bite to completely pass into the stomach below the band. It is very important that you allow each bite to go past the band before you take another bite. Therefore, there needs to be a full minute between bites. This is very slow eating. It takes commitment and practice. It is not easy, but is probably the most important of all the steps in eating with the LAP-BAND™.

GENERATING THE SIGNALS FOR SATIETY

The band generates background satiety and early satiation after eating. This is only the case when the band is adjusted to the correct level, when you are in what we refer to as the Green Zone. When the band is too loose, you are in the Yellow Zone. When it is too tight, you are in the Red Zone. The Green Zone chart is so important that we have given it pride of place on the inside back cover of the book. We want you to understand what it means and be able to guide us as to where you feel you are on the chart. A guide to the Green Zone chart is provided in Chapter 9 on page 194.

SATIETY SIGNALLING

When satiety and early satiation are being achieved, signals are passing from the stomach area to the hypothalamus indicating that there is no need for more food. This signalling is going on throughout the day to generate a sense of satiety and is augmented during eating to bring on early satiation (see Figure 4.6). It is important that we understand as much as possible about this signalling. We can then optimize the adjustments and the eating pattern. The better you understand satiety signalling, the better you will be able to work with the

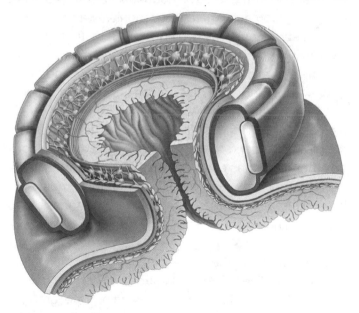

FIGURE 4.6 THE UPPER STOMACH HAS MANY NERVES THAT CAN DETECT AN INCREASE IN PRESSURE

band and to understand why the eating rules are as they are. We do not fully understand all the steps of this signalling process yet, but I believe that we are getting close.

Signals pass from the gut to the brain all the time and for many different reasons. These signals are carried by hormones or by nerves. A hormone is a small molecule that is generated in the gut and released into the blood-stream to travel to the brain. There it attaches itself to a receptor that is specific to that hormone and leads to an action. If a particular hormone from the region of the upper stomach where the band lies was generating the satiety signals, we would expect to find a higher level of that hormone in the blood throughout the day and there would be a special additional boosting of that level with eating. We have measured all the different hormones that we know come from that part of the stomach and find that the levels are not different in people with a band or without a band. Now, there could be other hormones coming from the upper stomach that we have not yet identified. But on current knowledge, it would appear that hormones are not responsible for the signalling.

The nerves from the stomach are much more likely candidates. There are thousands of nerves passing from the upper stomach to the brain. One group of these, the IGLEs, is our most favored candidate at the moment. IGLEs is an abbreviation of IntraGanglionic

Laminar Endings. These are very specialized nerve endings that lie in the wall of the stomach. When you squeeze or stretch the stomach, the IGLEs report that to the brain via the vagus nerve. They are the ones that, before you have a gastric band, detected that you had eaten enough or maybe too much. The band stimulates these special nerve endings by compressing the wall of the stomach. The brain thinks the stomach is full of food and turns off the hunger signals. If the band is adjusted optimally, there is a continuous stream of signals from the IGLEs to the brain, creating the background satiety. When part of a bite of food is squeezed across the band, an extra burst of signals passes up. If one bite of food requires up to six squeezes to get it across the band, then six additional bursts of signals can be generated for just the one bite. A meal of 20 bites provides sufficient additional input to the hypothalamus for early satiation.

And so the importance of the correct level of adjustment becomes clear. It provides the right level of signalling for background satiety. And it means that small bites of food, chewed well and then squeezed across the band, generate sufficient further signals to generate early satiation. "Eat a small amount of good food slowly" is the central rule of eating after the band. Hopefully, it is now clear why that rule is so important.

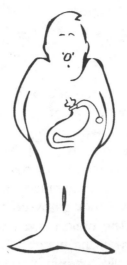

CHAPTER 5

THE LAP-BAND™: IS IT THE BEST OPTION FOR YOU?

KEY POINTS

- The LAP-BAND™ works primarily by inducing a sense of satiety.

- Its best features are its adjustability, truly minimally invasive placement and reversibility.

- The LAP-BAND™ treatment of obesity is a lifetime process, not just a procedure.

- It is extremely safe but does carry some risks and a significant "maintenance" requirement.

- The LAP-BAND™ is the best option for obese people who have failed non-surgical treatments.

FOUR PRINCIPAL FEATURES

Four principal features of the LAP-BAND™ overcome the dilemmas that are present with procedures such as gastric bypass and other methods of stomach stapling. These are outlined below.

1 THE LAP-BAND™ INDUCES SATIETY

The LAP-BAND™ works primarily by inducing a feeling of satiety, a feeling that you are not hungry. Even if you have not been eating for a prolonged period you do not feel hungry. You will wake up in the morning not feeling hungry. Food is no longer as central to your life as it once was.

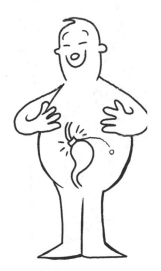

When you do eat, you will get a sense of satiation after a small amount of food and so will not feel the need or wish to eat much at each meal. You will not feel as hungry between meals. The net result is that you will be happy to eat just three or fewer small meals per day with no eating between meals. This is discussed in detail in Chapter 4, and the mechanism of how these effects are achieved is explained.

2 THE LAP-BAND™ IS ADJUSTABLE

This is perhaps the most attractive aspect of the LAP-BAND™. The sense of satiety is induced by the band pressing onto the surface of the stomach. By adding

or removing fluid from the band we can increase or decrease this sense of satiety. At operation we usually place the band with just a basal amount of additional fluid (3–4 mL). The tightness of the band, and therefore the level of satiety, is achieved by injecting some fluid through the skin into the access port tucked away under the fat of the abdominal wall.

This adjustability gives us control. Months or years after the procedure we are still able to modify the degree of satiety, so that we can gently find the level that enables us to achieve the weight loss we want without creating too many unpleasant symptoms.

3 THE LAP-BAND™ IS TRULY MINIMALLY INVASIVE

LAP-BAND™ placement is a much less invasive procedure than all other forms of gastric weight-loss surgery. The band can almost always be placed laparoscopically (by keyhole surgery) by passing some tubes through the skin and doing the operation through those tubes. This avoids any large incision, it avoids a lot of the handling of the gut, and it avoids much of the pain that goes with an open operation. And it is an outpatient procedure. All of our patients at "True Results" in the US have been treated as outpatients, over 20,000 of them. They generally leave the hospital about 2 hours after the band is placed. This illustrates just how gentle it is. No other weight-loss surgery could be done as an outpatient procedure.

This gentleness enables you to get back to your normal activities more quickly than you could after other procedures. Furthermore, there is very little trauma to the tissue inside the tummy when placing the band. There is none of the cutting of organs and stapling things together that is needed for the other surgical procedures for weight loss.

4 THE LAP-BAND™ IS REVERSIBLE

We have no intention of reversing the procedure. If we did reverse it and took no other steps, your weight would rise. However, there are situations where you may wish to have it reversed and it is nice to know that this can be relatively easily done. If the band is placed laparoscopically it can be removed laparoscopically and, as nothing permanent has been done to the stomach, it will return to its normal shape.

If, therefore, in 20 years time a new magical cure for obesity is invented that is much simpler, then the band could be removed and the new treatment applied.

THE LAP-BAND™ IS A PROCESS, NOT JUST A PROCEDURE

The excellent results that we have been able to achieve with the LAP-BAND™ are a team effort.

It is most important that we all see the use of the LAP-BAND™ in weight loss not just as an operation but as a process of care by a team, which commences before the band is placed and continues permanently thereafter. The surgeon, who is the leader of the team, and you, the patient, are the two key participants.

There must be a partnership between you and your surgeon. Success will only occur if both partners contribute. The surgeon must fulfill his or her responsibilities and you must fulfill your responsibilities. The surgeon must place the band accurately, securely and safely.

The surgeon must also ensure that you are able to access a comprehensive and expert follow-up process and must be sure you fully understand your role in the partnership. You, in turn, must be committed to following the rules about eating, exercise and activity, and you must always keep in contact with the medical team.

You should not consider having the LAP-BAND™ procedure unless you are totally committed to fulfilling your part of the partnership.

The rules about eating and exercise are discussed in more detail in Chapters 7 and 8. The essence of these rules is that you must have a maximum of only three small, good-quality meals each day with no snacks between. Each meal has to be solid food. The procedure does not work for liquid calories, so all liquids taken have to be of insignificant calorie content, such as water, mineral water, tea, coffee and low-calorie soft drinks. You must eat food that has good protein content, such as meat, egg dishes, dairy products, beans and lentils, and food that has high fiber content, such as vegetables and fruit. You must limit food that is high in fats and especially avoid food that contains simple sugars. Most importantly, you must learn to eat slowly and to eat a very small volume of food at each meal.

You must not only decrease your food intake but also increase your energy output. There must be an increase in activity and you should undertake a regular exercise program as well as always seeking to be active rather than inactive throughout the day.

The primary focus of the LAP-BAND™ effect is on the amount of weight that is lost. We expect that, on average, people who have the procedure will lose between one half and two thirds of their excess weight. For example, if your current weight is 250 lb (115 kg) and your ideal weight is 130 lb (60 kg), then you have a total of 120 lb (54 kg) of excess weight. One-half of this is 60 lb (27 kg) and two-thirds is 80 lb (36 kg). Therefore, typically your weight would come down to somewhere between 170 and 190 lb (78 and 87 kg).

This is the average. Some people will have more weight loss than this and some will have less, but on average this is what we expect. We want this weight loss to occur slowly and gently. We are quite happy for you to achieve the loss of two-thirds of excess weight by 1 to 2 years after the procedure. Because we now have control of your appetite, we are confident that even in later years we can still achieve further weight loss. Our aim is therefore to achieve the weight loss without interfering unnecessarily with quality of life. We don't want vomiting and we don't want too severe a restriction on the normal living pattern.

The loss of up to two-thirds of excess weight is our first target. We find that if this amount of weight is lost, most of the problems associated with obesity have been solved. We can have you go on to lose a greater amount of weight if there is a good reason. For example, if you have type 2 diabetes, the more weight you lose, the less likely it is that your diabetes will come back. We would therefore seek as low a weight for you as possible. It is important to realize, however, that we are not aiming primarily to achieve some ideal weight. We are aiming to solve the problems that the obesity causes.

Thus, we find that in association with this weight loss many people have major improvements in their medical problems. Diseases such as diabetes, asthma, high blood pressure, back pain and other joint pains, and heartburn are greatly improved in association with the weight loss. We have measured all of these effects in many of our patients and the outcomes are summarized in Chapter 2.

Also, people become much more physically active and more flexible. They are more confident and outgoing socially. Employment prospects are improved, not only because of improved physical appearance, but also because of much-improved capacity for physical activity and improved self-esteem and self-confidence. The self-hate of low self-esteem gradually dissipates as you realize that you are not such a bad old stick after all.

These multiple health, physical and psychosocial effects change your life. From feeling trapped within an obese body with its various problems, you quickly realize that

you can live a life without the illnesses and the limitations you have had. You quickly see that this procedure
really does work. It works without hurting you and it
works over a prolonged period of time. You achieve a
feeling of confidence that the problem is controlled.

NOW, WHAT ABOUT THE BAD NEWS?

It can't all be good news. There must be dangers, there
must be problems, there must be failures. What are the
bad things that can happen?

There are negative aspects to operations for obesity in
general and to LAP-BAND™ placement in particular,
and it is essential that you are aware of these.

DEATH

Any stomach operation for obesity is major surgery and carries with it the risks that would go with any complex operation. People have died from having operations for morbid obesity—it happens rarely with LAP-BAND™ placement, but we can never take away the risk completely. If you are older and if you already have certain diseases due to your obesity, or if you are otherwise unwell, you will be at greater risk.

Deaths associated with obesity surgery occur mostly because of heart attacks after the operation, clots passing to the lungs or infection due to the breakdown of some part of the stomach wall. The LAP-BAND™ has been shown to be very much safer than the stapling operations, but still death is possible. If we look at the figures for LAP-BAND™ placement across the world there has been about one death for every 2,000 to 3,000 people who have the procedure. This is less than one-tenth of the risk of death associated with gastric bypass[12] or biliopancreatic diversion. For a death to occur, multiple things have to have gone wrong and to have gone wrong in a particular sequence.

Firstly, it is extremely unlikely that anyone would die while under anesthesia. Our patients probably worry about this possibility the most and yet it almost never happens. Today, the knowledge base of anesthesia, the training and quality of our anesthetists and the presence of sophisticated monitoring systems make having an anesthetic very much safer than 50 or even 10 years ago.

If someone did die after a LAP-BAND™ procedure, a series of technical errors usually would have taken place. The surgeon would have to have made a mistake, not recognized what error occurred, not recognized that you were becoming unwell, not thought of the possible causes nor the investigations needed in response, and not treated the problem correctly. That is not just one error, but a whole series of errors that all line up into one path.

Nevertheless, you must minimize this risk by ensuring that your surgeon is well trained, has extensive experience, publishes or can make available to you his or her outcome data, and can show you a track record of being safe. The placement of the LAP-BAND™ is very safe when done properly but its potential risks are higher when the surgeon is not well trained or proficient.

In the 17 years of personal experience with the band and many thousands of people treated through our clinic, we have never lost anyone. We intend to keep it that way.

COMPLICATIONS

There is a very low likelihood of any postoperative problems, maybe one chance in 50 or less. Most are of minor significance and do not slow your recovery. Rarely, some can be of major significance and can be associated with a much longer hospital stay and a much longer recovery period. The sort of problems that do arise are infections that may occur in the lung, in the stomach in the area of the band, or at the sites where the ports are placed through the skin.

Clots can form in the legs and some of these can pass to the lungs, giving rise to the potentially dangerous situation of pulmonary embolism. The stomach can be damaged as the band is placed and perforation of the stomach can follow. Preexisting illnesses such as diabetes and asthma may become more difficult to manage around the time of the operation. We take a range of measures to reduce the likelihood of problems but, in spite of our best efforts, we are unable to promise that we can prevent them completely.

After the operation there is a period where a new eating pattern must be established and during this learning phase you may have episodes of vomiting. Ideally, there should never be vomiting after band placement. The force of vomiting can cause the stomach to shift its position within the band and the effectiveness of the band may be lost. We make special efforts to give instructions regarding eating and drinking to avoid vomiting, but this ideal cannot always be achieved.

LONG-TERM PROBLEMS

As with any complex system, there is a "maintenance" requirement with the band and, on our current figures, between 5% and 10% of patients will have something move or change or shift or break and will need to have this fixed by further surgery. Everything that can go wrong can be repaired, almost always by a laparoscopic approach. Three problems in particular that we should mention are enlargements of the small stomach above the band, erosions, and tubing or port problems.

Prolapse or slippage

The most common long-term problem that we have had after the LAP-BAND™ procedure is enlargement of the stomach above the band. This may occur because there has been slipping of the wall of the stomach through the band (prolapse or slippage) or because of stretching of the very small stomach (symmetrical enlargement).

At operation we place the band in a very particular position and we take special measures to fix it in that position. We also strongly encourage you to eat slowly and to take a small amount of food at each meal. Every time you eat you are going to create some stretching of the small stomach above the band. If you eat too quickly or you eat too big a meal you will create a much greater stretching. If, at the same time, there is an area of the stomach wall that has not been fixed adequately, that area can slip up through the band and create a pouch above it. We call this prolapse or slippage. If all of the stomach wall is well secured but you keep eating too fast or too much, over the months and years the small stomach will stretch and remain stretched. We call this symmetrical enlargement.

If a prolapse or symmetrical enlargement occurs, you will get heartburn and reflux of food and fluids. This is usually most noticeable at night. When you lie down the fluid and food that is sitting in the enlarged stomach above the band flows back up to the back of the throat. It is an unpleasant experience and can be associated with coughing and choking spells as some of the fluid trickles into the airway. If the enlargement of the stomach continues, it can eventually block off and cause vomiting.

If it happens and will not settle with removing some fluid from the band, it needs to be fixed. This can be done, but does require a further laparoscopic operation as a day patient or an overnight stay in hospital. You are then back on track and can continue with the weight-loss program.

When we compared the weight loss of those who have had a prolapse with our overall group of patients, there is no difference in the long term. It is like you were traveling down the highway making good progress. You were diverted onto a rough track for a period and, with the revision operation, we put you back onto the highway again. It has been very unusual for anyone to have a second slip.

The most important action you can take to avoid this problem altogether is to eat a small amount of good food slowly.

Erosions

It is possible for the band to work its way through the wall of the stomach until part of it lies within the stomach. This is known as erosion of the band and is now quite rare. If it does happen, the band ceases to be effective as it is no longer around the stomach and you will probably notice that you are able to eat a greater amount without that sense of restriction. It usually does not lead to any pain or acute illness. If an erosion happens we remove the band and repair the defect in the stomach. This may require an overnight stay in hospital. We may place a new band on a later occasion, usually after 3 months or more. This can all be done laparoscopically. Erosion was more common in our early experience with the band but has occurred in less than 1% of the people we have treated in the last 4 years and so is now a rare but manageable problem. In most cases we are unable to identify why it has happened and therefore we cannot share with you the secret for the increasing rarity of the problem. Hopefully, it will just go away completely and we may never know why.

Tubing/port problems

The tubing passing to the access port can break, particularly where it connects to the access port. Sometimes we miss the port in attempting to do an adjustment and hit the tubing with the needle. We use a special type of needle to make adjustments and, if the wrong type of needle is used, the access port can develop a leak. Sometimes the tubing can rub against something hard and wear through. If any of these problems arise, the access port needs to be changed. This is a minor surgical day-patient procedure but does require an admission to hospital and a general anesthetic. These problems are now increasingly unlikely to occur because of improvements in design and technique.

Considering and managing risk

The risk of death is very remote, the risk of complications at the time of LAP-BAND™ placement is minor, and the problems in the longer term have become quite unusual. Nevertheless, it is most important that you see the decision to go ahead with the LAP-BAND™ as a serious one that can only be justified if the problems associated with your obesity clearly exceed the problems that may be associated with the operation. You need to recognize your responsibilities to follow the rules and guidelines closely to minimize some of the risk of these events occurring.

FAILURE AFTER THE GASTRIC BAND

There can be failure to lose enough weight after the band. You may well have heard stories of the band failing, people just not losing enough weight or, when they have had good weight loss, regaining weight. You may have friends, relatives or acquaintances who have not had a good result with the band. You may have been told by your doctor that there is a question about the effectiveness of the band. You may have been told by a surgeon that they do not use the band because other surgeons have been unsuccessful or that they personally have not been able to achieve good results. These reports are all true. There are failures. Every medical treatment has a failure rate. Nothing is perfect and so, if people claim to you that they succeed with every patient, whatever the treatment is, either they are not following their patients very well or they are dishonest. Some level of failure is probably unavoidable. But many of the failures we hear about could have been quite easily avoided.

We define failure after LAP-BAND™ placement by three measures—inadequate weight loss, removal of the band and loss to follow-up. We measure our failure rate regularly. It is generally about 15% or one in seven who at any one time would trigger one or more of these criteria. Let's discuss each of these criteria in turn.

Inadequate weight loss

If we have not achieved loss of 25% of the excess weight by 2 years we regard that performance as inadequate and therefore a failure. On a number of occasions these patients are reasonably happy with their outcome. They may have lost 20% of their excess weight, their health is better and they are feeling improved. Nevertheless, we have to draw a line and we place it there. About 5% of our patients, one in twenty, have failed by this criterion.

We do not give up on these people. On the contrary, we are always seeking to achieve the best possible result for all our patients, and especially for these ones. We enter them into our "intensive care" program. We reassess them, their band, and their knowledge and compliance with the eating and exercise rules. We seek to diagnose what is wrong and then we seek to correct it. There may have been inadequate follow-up or adjustments. It may be that they are eating wrongly, or drinking multiple cans of soft drink or not exercising. It may be that there is a leak in the system or there has been a slip of the stomach through the band. We seek to identify the cause and then provide a period of intensive correction and follow-up to get them back on track. Nevertheless, at any one time, about a third of our patients in the "failure" group are those who have not lost more than 25% of excess weight.

It is important to realize that we do not give up on you because you have not lost enough weight and that those whose weight loss is less than we would like are commenced on our "intensive care" program.

There are three groups of factors that determine if failure will occur—band factors, patient factors and doctor factors. Unfortunately, when something doesn't work out well in medicine, doctors have a tendency to blame others. In this case they blame the band or they blame the patient. Most failures, however, are due to the doctor.

Band factors: We know that the band works well because of our own experience with thousands of patients, because of our own numerous research studies and because of the hundreds of publications attesting to its effectiveness. It works if it has been placed in the correct position and you are provided with the optimal after-care. On occasion, some part of the band might move or slip or break or change in some way that interferes with its effectiveness. These are real band factors in failure and we need to identify them early and fix them. But, in particular, we need the surgeon to avoid these events happening, to recognize them when they have occurred, and to fix them quickly and competently.

Patient factors: You are our partner on this journey. I have a clear set of responsibilities and you have a clear set of responsibilities. These are listed on page 118.

In essence, you must follow the eight golden rules (Chapter 11 and the DVD), which encompass all that we want you to do as your half of the partnership. You must follow the five golden rules regarding eating. You must follow the two rules regarding exercise. And you must always come back to the aftercare. No one is perfect and no one will follow all of those rules all of the time. But the closer you follow them, the better the outcome you will have. If you repeatedly ignore them, you will not achieve a good outcome. You will be at risk of joining the failure group. Gastric banding is strongly influenced by the quality of the contribution by both partners. You must be committed to your half of the partnership. You must be determined to fulfill your three requirements. If you are committed to achieving an optimal outcome, we can help you. If you are not so committed, there is no point undergoing the procedure. The band makes it easy for you. That is its role—to facilitate good eating (rules 1–5). As you lose weight you can increase your exercise and activity (rules 6 and 7). You don't have to do it all by yourself. With optimal adjustment, the band makes following the rules easy. But you need to make the commitment to following those rules and you must fulfill that commitment.

Doctor factors: By "doctor" I mean the full medical team. It may include the surgeons, other physicians, nurses, nurse practitioners, physician assistants, dieticians, psychologists and others. We have to place the band in the correct position safely, we have to make sure you have permanent access to good-quality after-care and we have to make sure that you have the information and understanding required to fulfill your part of the partnership. The failures after gastric banding are more related to these "doctor" factors than the patient or band factors. Most particularly, the aftercare is essential to achieving a good outcome. It must be correct at each visit, there must be enough visits to achieve an optimal outcome and the visits must continue permanently. In the reports of "disappointing" results after gastric banding, the quality of the aftercare is poor or is not even mentioned, as if the doctors did not realize it really mattered.

Selecting your surgeon: Be sure your medical team has good knowledge and experience in placing the band and has a real commitment and the capacity to provide an optimal aftercare program for you. You are then on your way to an excellent outcome.

The reports of "disappointing" results after gastric banding are usually on small series at the bottom of the surgeons' learning curves. The poor results may reflect a lack of good technical skills at laparoscopic surgery, lack of good training in the procedure and lack of good follow-up of their patients. An unusual or unknown type of band may have been used. You must go to a surgeon who has been able to achieve good results and is proud of the outcomes. Be wary of those who try to talk you into a stapling procedure such as gastric bypass or sleeve gastrectomy. They will try to tell you that the band doesn't work, that you are not suitable for the band or that it causes all sorts of problems. Generally, it means that they are not confident in performing the procedure competently or that they do not want to provide the follow-up care that is so important with the LAP-BAND™.

Do not be afraid to ask your surgeon about his or her experience and outcomes. How many patients have they treated? Have any died? What complications have occurred? What weight loss has been achieved? How many patients have been lost to follow-up? What facility is available to provide permanent and high-quality aftercare? It is your life being put at risk. And it is your health and lifestyle benefit that is missed if optimal care is not provided.

Removal of the LAP-BAND™

We have removed the band in just over 3% of our patients. In the early days of our experience we sometimes removed the band for prolapse or erosion. This would not happen today. We have the occasional patient who asks for the band to be removed because they do not feel it is helping them enough or they do not like the effect that it is having in some way. We discuss the decision with them carefully and if they are clear that they want it removed and they understand that their weight is likely to return to its initial levels, we will take it out. It is easy to do and if, years later, they wanted it back in again, we would be prepared to at least discuss that option. There is nothing irreversible about the placement or the removal.

Loss to follow-up

We are very keen that no one should be lost to follow-up. Good follow-up is one of the key elements for success with the LAP-BAND™. When we eventually track down some of those who have been lost to follow-up we note that they are frequently associated with a poor outcome. As we cannot be sure, we count people lost to follow-up in our failure group. At most times we are able to track more than 90% of our patients, leaving less than 10% who are in the failure category because of loss to follow-up.

We work hard to minimize any loss to follow-up by stressing to you the key role that follow-up plays in the LAP-BAND™ process. We are totally committed to maintaining follow-up with you permanently. This will mean a visit at least once every 6 months.

We request a maximum time between visits of 6 months for a specific reason. A very small but definite loss of fluid occurs from the band. If you had 7.0 mL of fluid initially and we saw you again at 6 months, it is likely there would be about 6.7 mL or less present. You would need a small addition of fluid to get back to the correct level. Even with a loss of just 0.3 mL of fluid, you are likely to feel more hungry and to find that you can eat too easily. Weight loss will stop and you may start putting on weight. If you don't realize that this small loss of fluid is occurring, you could feel that it is your fault that the procedure is not working and be hesitant to come back because you see yourself as a "failure." Please don't let yourself think this way. You must come back so that we can help—by adjusting, advising, educating and sharing information.

There is a greater risk of loss to follow-up if you move interstate or overseas. If you do, please contact your surgeon with your new address and please provide your surgeon with brief information on your progress as an absolute minimum. Almost always, they will be able to introduce you to a physician in your new country or region who can continue with your care. The LAP-BAND™ procedure is not just an operation; it is a partnership with the medical team in a lifetime process. You should only decide to go ahead with the procedure if you are prepared to make a commitment to this partnership and you must maintain this partnership by being in contact with us, or our colleagues, permanently.

There is an additional advantage in maintaining contact with us. It could be that reasons will develop in the future, either for you as an individual or for all people who have the band, which make it appropriate for some action to be taken. For example, we could find out something about the band that is so concerning that we recommend it be removed. The LAP-BAND™ is made of silicone and there are no known side effects of having this material within the body. We have now had over 17 years of experience with the LAP-BAND™ and its placement. There have been no long-term harmful effects as long as the position is correct and you are following the rules. We will continue to monitor each person and the information about the procedure itself and, as long as we maintain contact with you, we can always advise you of any new developments. On the positive side, maintaining contact allows us to bring you up to date with the latest information on how to get the best results from the band. We are always learning and we want to be able to share any new knowledge with you.

WHO IS CONSIDERED SUITABLE FOR THE LAP-BAND™?

We take four factors into account when determining whether this might be an appropriate procedure for you. These are the current level of your weight, the problems that this state of obesity generates, confirmation that you have made a significant effort at weight loss by other means, and the confidence we have that you understand what you are getting yourself into and have the commitment to fulfill your part of the partnership.

We discuss these in a bit more detail below.

1 YOU ARE OBESE

Obesity is a disease in our community when the body mass index (BMI) is greater than 30. A BMI of 30–35 is

described as mild-to-moderate obesity. A BMI greater than 35 is described as severe obesity. Before 2006, we would not wish to go ahead with the procedure if the BMI was less than 35. At a BMI of 35 or greater there is a clear risk to a long, healthy life, there are generally significant problems associated with obesity and there is known to be a poor outcome from any alternative therapy.

In 2006, we completed a major study of people with a BMI of between 30 and 35, and found that those who had the LAP-BAND™ had much better weight loss, improvement in health and improvement in quality of life than a matched group who had the best program of non-surgical treatment that we could offer.[13] We are, therefore, now prepared to accept people into the program with mild-to-moderate obesity, particularly if there are medical problems associated with the obesity or if it is clear that serious and multiple attempts to lose weight have been made by non-surgical means before seeking the LAP-BAND™.

2 THE OBESITY IS ASSOCIATED WITH PROBLEMS FOR YOU

If there is not a problem then we don't need to look for a solution. Even if you are truly morbidly obese by our definitions, we would not wish to proceed with any treatment unless you perceived a significant problem with your obesity. This might include the physical limitations, social isolation and the medical diseases that go along with morbid obesity. It may be a fear of the effects of your obesity on your future health and life expectancy. It must be the solution that you are seeking in answer to your problems. It is not something for us to encourage just because we perceive that you have a problem.

3 YOU HAVE MADE A SERIOUS EFFORT TO LOSE WEIGHT

It is important that you have made a significant effort to reduce your weight over a prolonged period of time. The effort is likely to include supervised diets and exercise programs and we find that almost all of our patients have spent considerable time and money with the commercial weight-loss groups in an attempt to lose weight. Most have tried some or all of the weight-loss pills available and many have been to some of the various health professionals who offer "solutions" to obesity. These include dieticians, naturopaths, hypno-therapists, acupuncturists and psychologists.

We do not make this stipulation because we believe that these alternative lines of therapy are effective. In fact, we know from numerous studies and you know from your own experience, they are almost always ineffective in the medium term. We make the requirement because it is an expression of your commitment to lose weight and without that commitment we cannot be confident that you will follow your half of the partnership.

4 YOU UNDERSTAND THE POTENTIAL BENEFITS AND RISKS, AND CAN FULFILL YOUR HALF OF THE PARTNERSHIP

Your weight status, the problems associated with your weight and your efforts to reduce your weight in the past are the main measures that we make. However, in addition, we will only proceed if we believe that you understand how your obesity is a problem for you, what the procedure consists of and what are realistic expectations of what it can do and what the risks are, and that we feel you are able to fulfill your half of the partnership. This book and the DVD of "The Eight Golden Rules" are important parts of the information sharing.

The whole process of the placement of the LAP-BAND™ and the follow-up process after the procedure is a partnership between you and us. We are committed to do all that is necessary to get the best possible result for you and you must be committed and able to fulfill your part of the partnership. For this we need to be sure that you have a realistic understanding of the potential benefits and risks, and of your responsibilities with regard to eating pattern and exercise.

Fulfilling the partnership

The surgeon has three commitments to fulfill their half of the partnership and the patient has three commitments to fulfill the other half.

SURGEON'S THREE COMMITMENTS

1 To place the band correctly and safely.

2 To ensure the patient is able to access good follow-up.

3 To teach the patient the rules to follow to fulfill their role.

PATIENT'S THREE COMMITMENTS

1 To follow the rules regarding eating and drinking.

2 To follow the rules regarding exercise and activity.

3 To come back for follow-up permanently.

DECISION-MAKING TIME

Here and in Chapters 1–3 we give you a wealth of information that should be helpful in making a decision. We have explained how obesity is a common problem that causes many other problems to your health, quality of life and survival. We have explained the benefits of weight loss, with improvement in health and happiness and the likelihood of increased survival. Most of this information is derived from published studies of our own patients.

We have explained the different options available to treat the problem of obesity, their strengths and their weaknesses. In particular, we have given you much information on the LAP-BAND™.

We have given you a list of criteria that you could apply to decide which of these options is the best for your problem. It is now time to apply those criteria to the different options we have discussed and to see if the LAP-BAND™ stands out as the best mix of effectiveness, safety and acceptability for you.

Table 5.1 summarizes the outcomes from each of the major options for weight reduction for each of the criteria. You will quickly see why the LAP-BAND™ is the preferred option.

TABLE 5.1 OUTCOMES FOR THE MAJOR OPTIONS OF WEIGHT REDUCTION

Attribute	LAGB	RYGB	BPD	SG
Safety	Very safe	Fair safety	Fair safety	Fair safety
Effectiveness— short term	Good	Good	Very good	Good
Effectiveness— long term	Good	Good	Good	Poor
Side effects	Few	Few	Moderate	Few
Adjustability	Yes	No	No	No
Reversibility	Easy and total	Very difficult	Difficult	Not reversible
Minimal invasiveness	Very gentle Outpatient	Not so gentle Inpatient	Not gentle at all Inpatient	Not so gentle Inpatient
Need for revision	May need revision	May need revision	May need revision	May need revision

LAGB = laparoscopic adjustable gastric banding, such as the LAP-BAND™; RYGB = Roux-en-Y gastric bypass; BPD = biliopancreatic diversion; SG = sleeve gastrectomy

Table 5.1 highlights the key advantages of the LAP-BAND™ over other surgical options—it is effective and yet safe; it is adjustable and reversible.

On the basis of this type of analysis, our extensive clinical experience with the LAP-BAND™ and, before that, with the gastric bypass, our awareness of the excellent outcomes that our patients have been able to achieve by using the band and the results of our numerous research studies, which have carefully and fully documented these benefits, we use the gastric band as the primary approach for achieving substantial weight loss.

We recommend the LAP-BAND™ as the best weight-loss procedure for the person who is obese, who is having problems arising from the obesity, who has tried the non-surgical options, who understands the rules for the band and who is committed to fulfilling their half of the partnership. If you feel that person is you, then go for it.

PATIENT ANECDOTE
BROOKE LINDSEY

I am 26 years old and I am a registered nurse. I have lost 152 lb (69 kg) since my LAP-BAND™ surgery. I have not had plastic surgery before or since my weight-loss surgery. I opted for weight-loss surgery after trying a number of other methods. I tried several commercial weight-loss programs, exercise, counting calories and fat grams, and memberships at gyms. I had success with the other methods, but none of them worked long term. ▸

I was tired of living life at 292 lb (133 kg). I had a son whom I did not want to embarrass one day. I wanted to be around to enjoy him growing up, to see him graduate and get married. I wanted to be healthy; however, the cosmetic change was a wonderful side effect. I wanted the woman on the outside to match the one on the inside. I chose the LAP-BAND™ because it was so safe. You can bet as a nurse I researched as much as I could. I loved the fact it was adjustable. If I was sick or wanted to have another child it could be adjusted and I could get the extra nutrition that I needed. I liked the idea of a slower weight loss also. I had heard with every diet I had ever been on that slower is safer.

LAP-BAND™ PLACEMENT: BEFORE, DURING AND AFTER THE PROCEDURE

CHAPTER 6

KEY POINTS

- Before placement of the LAP-BAND™ we will do a careful evaluation of your health.

- The procedure is almost always done laparoscopically and takes less than 1 hour.

- You should be out of bed, walking around and drinking water easily 1 hour after the procedure.

- You take liquids only for the first week, soft foods for the second and third weeks and then solid foods after that.

- You will return for the first adjustment of the band at about the end of the fourth week.

BEFORE THE OPERATION

After we jointly make the decision to go ahead with the procedure we will arrange for you to have some preliminary tests to document your general state of health. We may also do some specific measures of your current health problems and we will do some further tests that will minimize any risk associated with anesthesia. You will generally come into hospital on the morning of the procedure. The operation is performed under a general anesthetic and you are asleep for about 1 hour.

THE OPERATIVE PROCEDURE

The operation is almost always done laparoscopically. That means that we do not make any large incision. We pass fine tubes through the skin into the abdominal cavity. Mostly these are 0.2 in (5 mm) across, about as wide as a pencil. A special telescope is placed through one of these tubes. It has a camera attached to it so that we can see the inside of the abdomen by looking at a video screen. We pass surgical instruments through the other tubes to do the operation and we watch what we are doing on the video screen.

The band is placed around the upper part of the stomach so that there is almost no stomach above the band

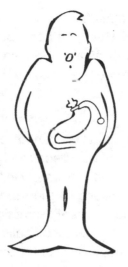

as shown in Figure 4.4 on page 82. Essentially all of the stomach is lying in its normal place below the band. We want each bite of food to pass down the esophagus, through the small cuff of stomach above the band, across the band and into the main stomach before you have another bite.

An access port is placed in the abdominal wall, usually slightly to the left of center, at about the belt line. Figure 4.1 on page 72 shows the access port at the end of the tubing. We can put a needle through the soft center of the access port to add saline to tighten the band. To place the access port we make a small cut in the skin, which measures 1.5 in (4 cm) in length.

At the end of the operation, you will note this small cut and also the sites where the ports passed through the skin. As the other ports are about as thick as a pencil, these incisions are quite small and, after healing, they can be almost invisible.

Occasionally, the operation cannot be performed laparoscopically. This may be because the liver is too large or there has been previous surgery in the area and there are too many adhesions of the organs to each other from some previous surgery. Sometimes, although we start the procedure laparoscopically, it may be more appropriate to change to an open operation. This may be because of a significant amount of bleeding or difficulties in passing the band around the stomach. You won't know that we have had to do this until after the completion of the operation, and you have to go into the operation recognizing that this may happen. On current experience, this will occur in less than one in 500 operations if there has been no previous surgery in the region.

If we need to do an open operation, generally you will have more discomfort after the operation and you will need to stay in hospital a day or two longer. Also, it will be longer before you are able to return to your normal activities. However, the procedure itself is done in essentially the same way and the end result is the same.

AFTER THE OPERATION

When you wake up from the operation you will feel some discomfort. There are two main sources of this discomfort. Firstly, the sites where we passed the tubes through the abdominal wall can be sore, especially the one where the access port is placed.

Secondly, it is common to have pain at the left shoulder area. This pain is actually coming from the diaphragm, which is the large sheet of muscle that separates the chest, with its heart and lungs, from the abdomen. It is called referred pain because, although it comes from the diaphragm, the brain interprets it as coming from the left shoulder and you feel sore there. It is common early after the operation but usually settles later that day or in a few days. Occasionally it can linger on for many weeks. We do not know exactly why it occurs and therefore we cannot predictably avoid it. Apart from letting time pass, various simple techniques have been found to help and are worth trying:

- hot packs to the shoulder
- standing or sitting upright
- resting quite still for 10 minutes
- walking about
- peppermint tea
- simple pain relievers—acetaminophen (paracetamol) or soluble acetylsalicylic acid (aspirin).

Although placement of the LAP-BAND™ is not totally painless it is not nearly as painful as if we had made a large incision. The anesthetist will have given you pain relievers before you wake up to block some of the pain and we can give you whatever additional treatment you need for pain relief at any stage. However, we will be trying to avoid too many pain relievers, especially opiate-type drugs such as morphine or meperidine (pethidine), as they can make you feel sleepy and nauseous. They can also lead to vomiting, which we certainly do not want.

You will be able to start taking fluids such as water, tea or coffee as soon as you are fully awake from the anesthetic.

You will have an intravenous drip in one arm to give you additional fluids and we are happy to remove this as soon as you are drinking fluids without difficulty. Generally, we expect to remove the intravenous drip about an hour after you come back to your bed from the operating room.

We will be encouraging you to get up out of bed and move around soon after the operation itself.

Normally, you will get out of bed and go for a brief walk within an hour of returning from the operating room.

If you do this, your recovery is likely to be smoother and easier and it is less likely that you will have problems with pain from then on. The nurses will encourage you and help you with this early mobilization.

Depending on where you are being treated, you may go home within 2 to 3 hours of the procedure or you may stay overnight. In the US and in Canada, it is usual to go home within 2 to 3 hours. This pattern has been followed in many tens of thousands of patients and has been shown to be very safe and generally preferred by the patients. In Australia, we are more likely to keep you overnight but we are very happy for you to go home on the same day if you wish.

We usually do a limited barium swallow X-ray examination before you go, to check that the band is in the correct position and that there is an easy flow of liquid past the band. The barium swallow X-ray examination is not essential but does provide some helpful information and therefore we use it if the costs are low. In some settings it is quite expensive and then should be used only for selected patients. It involves taking just two or three mouthfuls of the barium. It does not taste great, but, with the small volume, you will cope. The X-ray serves to reassure us that the band is in the correct position, shows that there is free passage of fluid past the band and provides a useful baseline record of the position of your band in case there is any problem

in the future. We keep an electronic copy of this on LapBase, our computer record of your baseline and follow-up details. It enables us to compare this X-ray with any future studies.

Before you go home we spend some time going over the rules about eating, particularly for the next 4 weeks. We will make your initial follow-up appointments and we provide you with contact details should any questions arise once you are at home.

After you go home we would normally expect you to take 1 to 2 weeks to get back to normal activities. Even at this time, however, you may be feeling more tired by the end of the day and you will still be trying to identify the best practices for eating. Nevertheless, by this time you will clearly see that you are almost fully recovered from the procedure and will already be seeing some weight reduction. You can return to work when you feel strong enough. Some will be back at work in a day or two but most will stay off work for at least a week from the procedure. We are happy for you to drive your car once you feel that you can move easily without discomfort and you can rotate enough to see about you. Normally this would be day 3 or day 4 after the operation.

EXERCISE AND ACTIVITY

We want you to start increasing activity and exercising as soon as possible. There is no physical activity or exercise you can do which will harm the band or its placement. After a laparoscopic procedure there is no weakness of the stomach muscles and so you do not need to worry about creating a problem through too much early activity. As long as your activity does not cause undue pain, please be as active as possible, as early as possible. We set no limits. We rely on your common sense.

STARTING TO EAT AND DRINK AFTER THE LAP-BAND™

WEEK 1 AFTER OPERATION: THE "LIQUIDS ONLY" PHASE

Introducing fluids and then food correctly during the first few days and weeks after placement of the LAP-BAND™ is important to preserve the structure that we have created at operation. It is essential that we do not unduly stretch the new small stomach at this early stage, but allow it to settle in position and develop some adhesions around it, which will stabilize it for the future. This takes some time and therefore during the first week after the operation you must take fluids only and avoid taking any solid food.

The fluid should go through quite rapidly and therefore you will probably not feel full. If, however, you do feel uncomfortably full after taking a small amount of fluid, you must not take any more until that feeling has passed. You will notice that you have very little appetite or interest in food. That is what we wish to achieve, and the less food you have, the happier we are.

At each mealtime, you should take a small amount of fluid, wait to see if it leads to any discomfort and, if not, then proceed with more. This same rule will apply later on when you are on solid food.

Notice that at this stage you will be taking calorie-containing liquids. These will be discouraged once you have moved beyond this liquid phase, but they are accepted now to enable you to have some nutritional intake while at the same time not putting any stress on the system as the band settles into position. We will encourage you to continue with this pattern for at least the first week after operation.

During this time you should take no solid foods at all, as this could block the pathway through the band and lead to enlargement of the stomach above the band. This is a most undesirable outcome and needs to be avoided by staying on fluids.

As you settle into a pattern of taking fluids it is most important that you become careful not to stretch the small cuff of stomach above the band. This is unlikely, particularly with clear fluids, but it is something that you will always have to be conscious of avoiding. It is best to sip fluids, not gulp them down.

During this first week, some people experience some nausea, headaches, dizziness and lightheadedness. These symptoms are often settled with some calorie-containing liquids such as fruit juice or yogurt.

The rest of week 1

You will need to remain on fluids only for about 7 days after the operation. During this time we want the band to settle into position without any strain put upon it. We therefore encourage you to avoid any solid food in case this causes obstruction at the narrow opening into the rest of the stomach, and vomiting. It is most important throughout this period that you do not generate sufficient feelings of fullness to have to vomit as this could possibly lead to movement of the band in relation to the stomach.

An ideal fluid to take through the first week is Optifast™ or another form of very-low-calorie diet. These are nutritionally well balanced but low in energy without any of the sugars or fats of some other liquids you may choose. If you were taking Optifast™ before the operation to reduce the size of your liver, it is a good idea to continue with Optifast™ through this first week, if possible.

However, some people cannot cope easily with Optifast™ and so alternative liquid foods need to be taken. The types of fluids that could be appropriate during this time include:

soup: avoid those with lumps of vegetable or other food within them; if you are not sure, puree the soup in a food processor

yogurt: particularly low-fat forms

milk: low-fat forms only and without added flavoring

V-8: this vegetable juice is highly nutritious

eggnogs: or other liquid forms of egg

fruits: vitamized to liquid form

fruit juice: unsweetened

pureed food: satisfactory as long as they are liquid

fruit smoothie:
    200 mL low-fat milk
    100 mL low-fat yogurt
    0.22 lb (100 g) fresh fruit such as banana,
      strawberry, mango
    Chill all ingredients, combine in blender and
    blend until smooth. Serve chilled with ice. This
    gives about four serves.

- Please note that these liquid calories are not allowed after the early postoperative period. They are for the first week only.
- Try as much as possible to avoid fluids containing sugar and minimize high-fat fluids.
- Never drink sodas or soft drinks. Each can of soft drink has the equivalent of 10 teaspoons of sugar. Avoid them totally.
- Low-calorie soft drinks are allowed but let the bubbles settle before you drink or you may feel uncomfortable because of trapping of the gas.

Inevitably, with the reduced intake of food, there will be reduced bowel activity. Try not to be concerned as this is normal if roughage is reduced. If you are truly concerned, take one of the bulk-forming laxatives such as Metamucil™ or Normacol™, along with plenty of water. That should get things going again.

A reasonable test of the appropriateness of a fluid during this liquid phase is whether it can be sucked up through a straw. If it is too thick to do this, you probably should not be trying it yet.

If you are taking medication in tablet or capsule form during this time we suggest you try to swallow them intact initially. If there seems to be some difficulty in getting them down, you should crush them. Capsules should not be a problem as they melt at body temperature and release the medication. It is the larger tablets that are most likely to cause problems. If you do have to crush a tablet, you should check with your pharmacist first as crushing the tablet can interfere with its absorption into the body.

Drink as much water as you feel like drinking. We do not set any particular amount to drink per day. Let your thirst guide you. If you feel thirsty, drink plenty, but if you are not thirsty, there is no need to force it. We place no maximum or minimum limits on the amount of water, mineral water, tea or coffee you drink each day.

WEEKS 2 AND 3 AFTER OPERATION: THE "TRANSITION" PHASE

After the first week, we begin the transition from liquid food to solid food. We want to do this slowly, because vomiting could occur if you try to make the transition too quickly. Initially the liquid-type foods can be gently thickened up. Soups can become thicker, fruit and vegetables less pureed or vitamized, and you can start taking some softer foods such as eggs and the yellow vegetables. One Weetbix™ or equivalent might be a typical breakfast. If you add a lot of low-fat milk it becomes nearly liquid, and is appropriate at the start of this period. By the end of the 2 weeks you should be adding less milk so that it is much more like a solid meal.

FROM WEEK 4 ONWARDS: THE "SOLIDS" PHASE

After week 3 you should be on solid food, and normally you will stay on solids from then on. Some foods are more difficult to cope with than others. The foods that tend to be most difficult are bread, red meat and sometimes rice. White meats, particularly fish, are usually well tolerated, but initially it might be appropriate to prepare it with a sauce, then to leave out the sauce as you move to completely solid foods. By the end of the third week, you should be on solid foods and liquids-only will be in the past. There is one exception to this. If, due to illness or inadvertent error, you begin vomiting

and have some difficulties with solid foods, it is important then to go back initially to clear liquids and come
forward again through soft foods to solid foods. If this
happens, you should contact the clinic and check if
you need to be seen by one of the physicians.

Once you have established a diet based on solid food
you will stay with this permanently. From then on you
need to avoid taking any liquids that contain calories,
except for some low-fat milk and a glass or two of wine.
See the discussion of this on page 168. Limit your liquid
intake to water, mineral water, tea, coffee and low-
calorie soft drinks. Be careful initially with the carbon-
ated drinks. The gas can build up, as you cannot burp
as readily after band placement as before, and it can
be uncomfortable. See how you go, letting the drink go
fairly flat, and increase it if you do not have trouble. A
more detailed food guide is provided in Chapter 7.

There are two final important messages:

1   If at any time during the first few weeks, or indeed
    at any time in the years afterwards, you feel that
    there is something wrong, it is essential that you
    get a message to your surgeon about your worries.
    A number of bad things have happened to people
    after the LAP-BAND™ procedure because they
    have consulted with someone who is not famil-
    iar with the band and who then makes a mistake
    of diagnosis, or treatment, or both. We do want to

know if you may be in trouble. We would be very disappointed if you did not contact us and subsequently something serious happened that we might have been able to help you avoid. Almost always we can assure you that there is no problem. We are happy to do that, and it is much better than not hearing from you if there Is a real problem.

2   During the first week it is usual not to feel at all hungry, to be quite uninterested in food. Please remember that feeling. That is the feeling of satiety. That is what we want to achieve in the long term by adjusting the band. The feeling will fade away over the 4 weeks so that by week 4 you are usually getting hungry, the weight loss has stopped and the amount of food you are eating has increased. That is normal. We start to add saline to the system at that time and seek to move you back to the state of satiety that you had in the first week.

CHAPTER 7

EATING AND DRINKING AFTER THE LAP-BAND™

KEY POINTS

- The LAP-BAND™ facilitates good eating behavior.

- Eat slowly and a small amount at each meal.

- Eat a maximum of three meals each day.

- Do not eat anything between meals.

- Eat food that is high in protein.

- Do not drink calorie-containing liquids.

- Take a vitamin/mineral supplement.

THE KEY TO LOSING WEIGHT IS TO EAT LESS

Hundreds of books have been written by people giving you their "secret" for losing weight. In general, they talk about this type of food versus that type of food, this pattern of eating versus that pattern of eating, this mix of food versus that mix of food. Mostly, they are missing the point. The key to losing weight is to eat less. The amount of food is far more important than the type of food. The body can turn almost any food into whatever it wants. We will return to the types of food later on. Certainly some foods are preferred to others. But, at this point, please do not get lost in the detail of the type of food; focus principally on the amount of food.

We have no way of beating the laws of nature, and one of the laws of nature—the Law of Conservation of Energy—states that energy can be neither created nor destroyed. If you take in more energy (calories or kilojoules) than you use up, your body will store it, mainly as fat. If you take in less energy than you need, the body will use up some of its stored fat to provide that extra energy. To lose weight, you must reduce your energy intake or increase your energy output or, preferably, do both.

In Chapter 8 we look at how you can use up more energy by increasing activity and exercise. For now we will concentrate on the most important part of the equation—reducing your intake.

With the gastric band, you eat less. It allows you to eat less, it encourages you, it cajoles you, it seduces you to eat less. But it does not force you to eat less. It is not a barrier. It does not set fixed limits. You could easily beat the band if you chose to. It is a modifier of appetite. It is like having your own personal assistant watching over you all the time, helping you do the right thing.

THE LAP-BAND™ WORKS BY DOING TWO THINGS

Firstly, and most importantly, the LAP-BAND™ takes away the sense of hunger and replaces it with a sense of satiety.

We explained in Chapter 5 how the band generates a background of satiety, of not being hungry throughout the day. By gently compressing the top of the stomach it generates signals to the appetite center of the brain that all is well. There is no need for food. These signals are passing upward 24 hours a day. When the band is adjusted correctly, you will not feel hungry. You will wake up in the morning, having not eaten for more than 12 hours, and not feel hungry. You will forget mealtimes. You will not spend hours every day thinking about food—what to have for lunch, what to buy for dinner, what you would like to have for a snack as you walk past a shop. You can get on with your day's activities without the distraction of food. We call this state of not being hungry, of having no appetite for food, as "satiety."

With this sense of satiety present most of the time, you will be happy to eat no more than three times a day. You must not eat between meals. No snacks or nibbles or just one biscuit with your coffee. If you are tempted to eat, resist it. If you cannot resist it, eat something healthy, like a piece of fruit or a raw vegetable like a bell pepper (capsicum) and come and tell us about it. It usually indicates that the band is not quite tight enough. A little added fluid to the band should reduce that hunger between meals.

We don't mind if you eat less often than three times a day. In fact we are pleased. Do not eat if you are not hungry. There is no need to eat because of the time of day or because you have not eaten for many hours or because your family are eating and want you to join them. Many of our patients do not feel like eating at breakfast time. They are happy to start the day with a cup of tea or coffee or just a glass of water. If you do not feel like having anything for breakfast, don't have anything. Don't believe the myth that breakfast (or any other meal) is important or essential or required for good health. Breakfast is a modern phenomenon. In the Stone Age, the hunter–gatherers did not eat breakfast.

It was not a part of the Stone Age diet. There was no food available each day until the hunters and gatherers went hunting and gathering.

The Stone Age man and woman could not be sure from day to day if there would be enough food. Over three million years they were programmed to cope with major variations in food intake. We all carry that same program. No significant change has occurred in this aspect of our genetic coding during the last 100,000 years. We are set up to miss meals, and we are able to miss meals. So don't fight it. With a little bit of help from the gastric band, you can enjoy it.

The second effect of the LAP-BAND™ comes when you do eat something. You will get a sense of satisfaction after a small amount of food.

After you eat a small amount, you will no longer feel the need for food and can stop eating. This is called "satiation," which differs from satiety in coming *after* eating. With correct adjustment of the band, the sense of satiation, of having had enough, should come after a very small volume of food, about the amount of food you could get into half a glass.

Half a glass of food! This may seem like a very small amount, but it happens to be about the right amount.

Please use "half a glass" as a concept of the amount you should eat at a meal, not as an actual measure. Half a glass is 125 mL in volume and equivalent to a weight of 125 g. We do not mean half a glass of shredded lettuce. We mean half a glass of solid food. All food has a high water content and some has lots of spaces of air. Fruit, in particular, is almost all water. Some vegetables and breakfast cereals are loosely packed with lots of air. If you are eating foods that are loosely packed you will need to estimate the compressed volume and adjust accordingly. Think more in terms of the weight of the food than its volume, keeping 125 g of weight in mind. If you are eating foods that are largely water, such as most fruit and many vegetables, you have to recognize that as you chew well and then swallow, the water will be released and passes on. For food such as meat, fish and cheese, the volume you see is the volume you get. For such food, 125 mL in volume will be roughly 125 g in weight. For fruit and vegetables, allow for some compression to adjust for the air spaces and water content.

HOW YOU SHOULD EAT

Use a small plate.

Put this small amount of food onto a small plate. The average dinner plate is far too big. You could feed a family with the food you could pile onto the average dinner plate. Use a small but elegant plate—an appetizer plate or bread and butter plate.

Take a small bite of food and chew it very well.

Always eat with a small fork or spoon. The amount of food that could be loaded onto a normal fork is too big for a single bite. It could stretch the space above the band and impair the squeezing of the bite across the band. An oyster fork is about the right size. Develop the habit of taking small bites. It has to become a part of your life. But see it as a positive thing. It provides the opportunity for you to enjoy food more than you ever have. I want you to eat the very best food. You can only eat a small amount, so you can now afford to buy the best. Quality in place of quantity. And look forward to enjoying the best. Enjoy the taste, the textures and the flavors of the food. So often we have no recall of the taste of meals. We shovel the food in, swallow it down and it's gone. I now want you to savor the qualities of the food. As you chew it well, think about these qualities and enjoy them. With the band, we want you to reduce the quantity of eating but we also want you to increase the quality of eating.

Make sure everything is reduced to a mush before swallowing.

You must not swallow lumps of food. All food must be chewed until it is the consistency of mashed potato. It should be broken into very small pieces, which, when mixed with saliva in the mouth, could be described as a mush or a slurry. There should be no lumps. Certain foods are difficult to reduce to mush. The two most common examples are red meat and bread. No matter how much you chew them, they tend to stay in one piece. Other foods to be careful with include pasta and rice.

If you cannot reduce a bite to mush, then spit it out. Don't swallow it. Think what could happen if you swallow a lump that cannot be squeezed past the band. The esophagus is capable of vigorous contractions. It will squeeze hard to get the lump through. That vigorous squeezing will cause discomfort. You will feel it at the top of the tummy and behind the sternum or breastbone. The esophagus will continue squeezing until it may eventually succeed in clearing the piece of food; or, more commonly, you will need to bring it up.

You will excuse yourself from the table, go to the bathroom and bring it up. It is not really vomiting, but better described as "hawking," a mixture of regurgitation and coughing. Not pleasant. Much better to avoid it.

Once you swallow the bite, wait a minute.

It is important to realize that there is no space left above the band for storing any food. Each bite must go through the band before you have another bite. What you have is a "virtual" stomach rather than an actual stomach. Look again at Figure 4.4 on page 82. It shows the lower part of the esophagus, a little stomach and then the band. The esophagus squeezes the food across the band. There is no small stomach, there is no mini-stomach; no storage space, no "pouch." As you eat, space for the food can only be created by stretching the virtual stomach that is there and the esophagus above it. Each bite of food must be small. And each small bite of food should be allowed to go completely through the band before you take another bite. We want to avoid too much stretching or too rapid stretching. If you eat too quickly or take too big a bite, you will stretch that area more than we like. If it is stretched, it cannot squeeze as effectively. Food can build up above the band and cause more stretching. If you do it repeatedly, three times a day for 1 or 2 years, you will develop a pouch above the band that does not empty properly. Reflux of the food into the back of the throat, heartburn and vomiting can follow, and we may then need to revise the position of the band. This is why we constantly stress the need to eat slowly and eat a small volume of food.

It takes time for the esophagus to squeeze the food across the band: up to a minute when everything is working well, and maybe longer than a minute if you have stretched the area above the band. A minute is a long time to wait, but this is what is required. You have to put down your fork or spoon and do something other than eat. Like talk with your family, read a page of a book, progress a little with the Sudoku puzzle or watch the news on television. But wait a minute between swallows. You can take another bite before the minute is up because you will be chewing that bite for maybe 15 to 20 seconds before it is chewed enough to be ready to swallow. But from one swallow to the next, wait a minute.

You must never feel full. You must stop eating when you are no longer hungry.

You must learn to recognize the feeling of satiation so that you know that you have had enough. This sense of satiation is different from what you have previously experienced. It is not the feeling of being full. You will get that feeling of fullness if you have been eating too fast or too big a bite. You have food building up above the band and there is stretching of the virtual stomach and the esophagus. We want to avoid ever getting to that point. It is an uncomfortable feeling. If it happens occasionally no harm is done but if it happens regularly you will eventually have permanent stretching above the band. You must try to avoid eating to a point where there is discomfort. Instead, you must stop when you are no longer hungry. As you contemplate the next bite, ask yourself, "Am I still hungry?", "Do I need that next bite of food?" Learn to detect your own particular signals of "enough" and "too much." Understand the sense of satiation, the sense that you are no longer hungry. Learn to stop eating with the first signal and try to avoid the second signal. The band has provided you with a "stop" button. Do not keep eating when it says stop. Discard the food that is left. No more eating until the next meal. Get on with doing something more useful than eating. Seek to never eat all the food on the plate. Develop this into a habit.

Our mothers taught us to eat everything on the plate and to stop fidgeting. Both pieces of advice were correct when food was in short supply, as was the case during the first half of the 20th century. You couldn't waste food as there was not enough of it. And they knew that fidgeting used up a lot of energy without serving a purpose. Wasting food and fidgeting were both ways of wasting energy when we didn't have enough. Now we have too much. Now we want you to leave food on your plate and, yes, you can fidget as much as you like—it is a great way of using up energy.

A normal meal should take 20 minutes or less. At the most, go out to 30 minutes. But do not sit there, eating slowly, and taking an hour or more. That defeats the purpose. If you are eating correctly and taking about one bite per minute, by 20 minutes you should have reached that point of satiation. If you find this is not happening, if you find you are wanting more, either you are eating foods that are too liquid and do not need the squeezing across the band or you need more tightening of the band.

Please be reassured and reassure those around you that you will not eat too little. We have measured the nutritional status of our patients very carefully over the past 12 years and we do not find that people become malnourished. It just has not happened unless there is something seriously wrong with the position of the band causing a blockage, and that blockage is not relieved for many months. In theory it could happen but, in reality, it has not. There is, therefore, no lower limit to your food intake. Some nutritionists and dieticians are very focused on what, in the US, are called the Dietary Reference Intakes (DRIs), and in Australia the Recommended Daily Intakes (RDIs). These cover the total energy (calories/kilojoules) and the macronutrients—the proteins, fats and carbohydrates that those of us who don't have a band should eat each day. We don't set minimum DRIs or RDIs for protein or fat or carbohydrates for patients with the LAP-BAND™. However, there are minimum requirements for some of the micronutrients, such as iron, calcium and vitamins. These latter can be met without any food, and are discussed later in the chapter.

Our golden rule number 1 is "Have a maximum of three small meals each day." If you are eating all the food on the plate, if you are feeling that you could do with a bit more, if you are looking for more food than we describe, if you are tempted to snack between meals, you must tell us. It is the signal that there may be a need for some further adjustment. The key benefit of the band is the ability to take away hunger. It will only do this if the adjustment is correct. You must call for help if you are wanting to eat too much or too often.

The "20–20–20, wait a minute" rule may be helpful to you. A meal should not last longer than 20 minutes, you should not take more than 20 small bites, you should chew each bite for 20 seconds, and you should wait a minute between each swallow.

WHAT YOU SHOULD EAT

What you should eat is less important than how much you should eat.

Before you start to worry about what you will eat, please never forget that the only way, ultimately, to lose weight is to eat less. The only way the band works is that it allows you to eat less. There has been so much said and written on individual foods, their benefits and their hazards—fats versus carbohydrates, saturated fats, trans-fatty acids, polyunsaturated fats, mono-unsaturated fats, omega-3 fatty acids, total cholesterol, "good" and "bad" cholesterol, high and low glycemic index foods, the good and bad effects of alcohol, and the need for dietary fiber. While there is good science supporting some of the claims of health benefit or harm, there are other claims where the evidence is rather soft, and there are some that require an act of faith, as there is simply no evidence or the claim even goes against the evidence.

It is not my purpose to enter the myriad of debates on good and bad food for the people of the world. That would be to step into a snake pit of conflict. But I *will* tell you what is important to you as a person with a gastric band. I will indicate what that small amount of food should look like to get an optimal result from the band. We want you to achieve the weight-loss targets but also to maintain a healthy nutritional status, to be free of symptoms or difficulties associated with eating and to enjoy a high-quality eating experience. As much as possible, the advice will be supported by good science, by the research that we have done or by the research studies of others. At times, we will have to resort to common sense. We will take each of the main components of food in turn and comment on how the patient with the LAP-BAND™ should think about it.

In general, we recommend an intake that is about half of what is generally recommended by various nutritional guidelines.

We base this on extensive experience of monitoring the achievement of weight loss in several thousand patients and identifying what appears to be an optimal food intake for weight loss without signs of nutritional deficiencies. In particular, in our clinics, we regularly measure protein levels in the blood, look for changes in bone thickness, check for anemia and low iron levels, and measure the levels of vitamin B12 and folic acid. We also closely monitor the general health of our patients, particularly documenting the improvements in the diseases that their obesity had caused. From all these measures we have not been able to identify any pattern of nutritional deficiency associated with the food intake pattern that we recommend.

TOTAL ENERGY

You should take less than 1,200 calories (5,000 kJ) per day. Initially you will probably take well below this, but when your eating pattern stabilizes, an intake of 1,000–1,200 calories (4,200–5,000 kJ) per day is probably about right. Because of the excess weight you are now carrying through the day, your total energy needs will be higher initially and come down as you lose weight. Eventually you achieve a balance between energy intake and energy use and your weight will stabilize at that new point.

Typically, you will lose 50 to 70% of your excess weight before you stabilize. You may lose 100% of your excess weight or you may lose only 30%. To a large extent, where you eventually stabilize will be a reflection of your total energy input. You have much more ability to vary this input than you do to vary the output. The band is there to help you reduce the input. The changes to the output (exercise and activity) are up to you.

We plan to work with you in getting your total energy input to less than 1,200 calories (5,000 kJ) per day. We can achieve this if the adjustment of the band is optimal (see Chapter 9) and you follow the guidelines about eating.

PROTEIN

Adequate protein intake is essential. Protein provides the key amino acids that you need to maintain the body—to build tissue, replace cells, make enzymes and hormones. The fats and carbohydrates are important as the fuel to run the body. But the protein provides the essential building blocks. You must get adequate protein as a first requirement. The fats and carbohydrates are the optional extras.

We estimate that patients eating optimally after placement of the band get about 30–40 g of protein per day. We have carefully monitored our patients' protein levels. None has developed protein malnutrition and so we are happy to encourage people to continue at this level. The best sources of protein are meats, particularly fish, shellfish and chicken. Other meats (beef and lamb) can be difficult to turn into mush in the mouth and so can cause trouble. Other good protein sources are eggs, milk and cheese, beans, lentils, soybeans and their derivatives, and nuts. In the half a glass or 125 mL, plan for at least a half to be a protein-containing food, with

say 60 g or more as a target. Sixty grams of fish provides approximately 14 g of protein. Two medium-sized
eggs weigh about 85 grams and provide 11 grams of
protein. Those options are a good start to a meal and to
the day's protein needs.

Fish is our favorite meal. It is nutritionally good, a soft
meat that is easy to break up in the mouth, it has wonderful flavors and is readily available. Prefer cooking by
steaming, poaching or grilling to frying. Avoid coatings
of batter or breadcrumbs. They simply push up the
calorie intake without any nutritional benefit. Shellfish
such as shrimp, prawns, crabmeat and scallops are
equally good. Chicken and other poultry, if kept moist,
can be tender enough. Red meats such as beef, lamb
or pork can be difficult for many because they can be
difficult to break each bite up in the mouth to make the
mush that we seek before you swallow. If you want to
try red meat, eat the very best, such as fillet steak or
rack of lamb, lightly cooked and cut into small pieces.
Then chew it well but don't swallow it until it is mush.

As you contemplate the half a glass of food for each
meal, always consider the protein-containing foods
first. Place enough of this food on your plate to fill half
of the symbolic glass. Next, add vegetables and fruit,
making some allowance for the air spaces and water
content. Starchy foods come in last, for whatever
space, if any, is left.

FATS

Fats and carbohydrates are the fuels that run the body. They provide the energy to keep the temperature normal, to enable the organs and systems to do their work and to allow the amino acids to be made into protein. About 70% of the energy we take in is used just to keep the body working. Even if we lay perfectly still all day, we would use up that energy. The other 30% is used to provide energy for the activities of daily living. This partly explains why exercise is a relatively weak method for achieving weight loss. Exercise affects just that last 30%.

Fats are the major source of energy. They are described as "energy dense" because you get approximately 9 calories (40 kJ) of energy from each gram of fat you eat, whereas you get only 4 calories (20 kJ) of energy from each gram of carbohydrates. Fats in the diet are made up of fatty acids linked together with glycerol. Some of these fatty acids are needed by the body because we cannot make them ourselves. You also get the fat-soluble vitamins—A, D, E and K—through eating fat. With any reasonable range of food intake you will still get enough of these, so don't base your plan for food for each day of each week on needs for them. Try to reduce fat intake where possible because of its energy density. Don't become obsessive about it, but do always prefer the low-fat options.

Fat has been getting bad press for the past 30 years, as it has been taught that eating fat has led to diseases of the heart and major blood vessels. Gradually, we are achieving a higher level of understanding of which fats are bad and which are probably quite helpful. Use the following as a guide:

1   Avoid too much of the saturated fats. These are generally derived from animal sources but also from coconut and palm oil. They tend to be solid at room temperature. Look for lean or fat-free meats. Trim off the excess fat from chicken. Prefer fish. But don't be too obsessed about the saturated fats. They are not as evil as they have been painted. They are an important part of many meats and add to the enjoyment of eating them.

2   Avoid the trans-fatty acids. They are associated with a higher prevalence of heart disease. They are generated in food processing when liquid vegetable oils are heated to become solid. Food processing companies like the trans fats because they are less likely to lead to the rancidity that occurs with oxidation of the unsaturated fats, and therefore food containing them stores longer. The trans fats provide one good reason to minimize your intake of processed foods.

3   In general, the unsaturated fatty acids are fine but some are better than others.

4   Among the good guys at the moment are the omega-3 fatty acids. Eating fish is the best way to get plenty of these. As fish is also our favorite source of protein, we are happy to encourage the omega-3 enthusiasm. You also get some of the omega-3 fatty acids in vegetable oils such as canola and soybean.

5   The other good guys are the monounsaturated fatty acids, as are found in olive oil. The "Mediterranean" diet has long been regarded as healthy, and olive oil appears to be an important contributor to its reputation. Canola oil contains these good fatty acids also.

CARBOHYDRATES

There are three forms of carbohydrates you need to consider—simple sugars, starches, and fiber.

Simple sugars

These are of no particular nutritional value and add calories. It is best to avoid them. This is particularly true of the table sugar variety, known as sucrose, that goes into so many foods and drinks. One hundred years ago we ate about 1 lb (500 g) of sugar per person per year. Now we eat over 150 lb (70 kg) per year, 150 times more. Simple sugars fill no particular nutritional need. They are empty calories. And as they don't need much digestion they are absorbed quickly, which pushes the blood sugar level up quickly. Thus, they have a high glycemic index. They are generally in liquid form. Any soft drink is an example of a bad liquid. A 13 fl oz (375 mL) can of soft drink contains the equivalent of 10 teaspoons of sugar. Other high-sugar foods become liquid as soon as you eat them. Chocolate and ice cream combine the evils of simple sugars with a high-fat, and therefore high-calorie, content and, being liquid, they give no sense of satiation. It would be best if you just leave simple sugars out of your diet altogether. Unfortunately, this is not always easy as food manufacturers add sugar to all sorts of foods to increase their popularity. So you need to watch out for them. Read the food labels for total sugar content. Even a glass of freshly squeezed orange juice has the equivalent of about 7 teaspoons of simple sugar. It is not much better than a soft drink. Don't drink fruit juice; we prefer you eat the fruit.

Starches

These are called complex carbohydrates, as opposed to the simple sugars, but they are just long chains of simple sugars strung together. The starches are the main form of carbohydrates that you eat. The common foods that are rich in starches are bread, potatoes, rice, pasta and cereals. These normally form a significant part of people's food intake each day. As soon as they get to the gut, they are broken down to their simple sugars and absorbed that way. We do not absorb anything larger.

Consider them an optional extra. There are no essential nutrients in the starches. They are fillers. A little starchy food as a part of a meal is probably okay but keep it to a minimum and do your best to drop it altogether. Life can go on very well without bread and breakfast cereals.

And they can be difficult to swallow after the band. Be careful with fresh bread in particular. It can tend to stick on the way down after band placement, as it is hard to break up into mush in the mouth. Older bread or toast may be fine. Rice and pasta can also be a problem for some. None is essential. Life will go on if you don't eat any of these foods. Use them sparingly.

Roughage

Complex carbohydrates, apart from the starches, are generally not absorbed by the body and are often referred to as roughage. They pass through the gut, largely intact and make up some of the bulk of the bowel motions. It has been argued that, as a population, we should have more roughage in our diets. I will not enter that debate and air my skepticism of some of the science behind it. I am happy for you to eat high-roughage foods, such as the leafy vegetables and occasional cereals, as long as you stay within the guideline of having the amount of food you can get into half a glass for each meal. Some people notice constipation early after band placement. Please avoid or solve this problem if it concerns you by using bulk-forming laxatives, as these are a pure form of roughage without any food value. Very few of my patients need to use them for long.

The glycemic index (GI)

This is currently a fashionable concept. The carbo-hydrates in food are broken down in the gut and absorbed as glucose. As the glucose is carried into the bloodstream, the level of it in the blood rises. The GI is a measure of the rate at which the food leads to increased glucose in the blood. A food is said to have

TABLE 7.1 FOODS RATED BY GLYCEMIC INDEX (GI)

Low GI foods (< 55)*	Medium GI foods (55–70)†	High GI foods (> 70)‡
Skim milk	Banana	Watermelon
Plain yogurt	Pineapple	Dried dates
Soy beverage	Raisins	Instant mashed potato
Apple/plum/orange	New potatoes	Baked white potatoes
Sweet potatoes	Popcorn	Parsnips
Oat bran bread	Split pea or green pea	Instant rice
Oatmeal (slow cook	soup	Corn Flakes™
oats)	Brown rice	Rice Krispies™
All-Bran™	Couscous	Cheerios™
Converted or parboiled	Basmati rice	Bagel, white
rice	Shredded wheat cereal	Crackers
Pumpernickel bread	Whole wheat bread	Jellybeans
Pasta		French fries
Lentils/kidney/baked		Ice cream
beans		Digestive cookies
Chickpeas		Table sugar (sucrose)

*Choose these forms of carbohydrates most often.
†Have modest amounts only.
‡Avoid these forms of carbohydrates.

a high GI if it is rated above 70, intermediate if it is 55 to 70, and low if it is below 55. We are still not at all sure whether the GI is of any importance for the patient with the LAP-BAND™, or for anyone for that matter. Until we know that it really matters, if you are going to eat one of the carbohydrate-containing foods, it is probably smart to focus on low GI foods as much as possible. Table 7.1 provides some examples of low, medium and high GI foods. More detailed listings are readily available elsewhere. Look at them but don't let them dominate your thinking. They are probably not all that important to your outcome after the band.

VITAMINS

There are 13 vitamins that humans need to maintain health. Vitamins are organic chemicals that we need for normal metabolism but we are unable to make within the body. We therefore have to be sure that we get sufficient levels of them with our diet, and we can take a multivitamin supplement to be sure. One of the attractive features of the LAP-BAND™ is that nutritional deficiencies are not expected. There is usually sufficient iron, calcium and vitamins in the food that you eat to maintain health. However, we do recommend that you take a multivitamin replacement just in case. This recommendation is most important for female patients who are menstruating or may become pregnant. Check that the vitamin and mineral preparation has folic acid present. You should be taking at least 400 micrograms of folic acid per day. Added iron, calcium and vitamin B12 are also desirable.

The fat-soluble vitamins—vitamins A, D, E and K—are usually not present in normal vitamin supplements. It is important to get enough vitamin D, about 600 international units (IU) per day, as a deficiency will impair absorption of calcium and may lead to osteoporosis, a thinning of the bones, later in life. One of the best sources of vitamin D is sunlight, so your 30–60 minute walk each day provides that important extra benefit. Milk and fish are other good sources of vitamin D. We are happy for you to take up to 1 pint (500 mL) of low-fat milk per day. You can add this to your cereal, tea or coffee or just drink it. And you already know that we are keen on fish as a key part of your food intake. A small serve can provide a tasty, interesting meal of protein, omega-3 fatty acids and vitamin D.

Even with a small food intake, you should be getting enough of the vitamins A, E and K with your food. The fat-soluble vitamins are stored in the body, so that taking too much can lead to harmful toxic effects. You should not take supplements of these vitamins without medical advice.

MINERALS

Adequate daily intake of minerals is just as important as vitamins.

Sodium and potassium are taken as a part of your food and fluid intake and we have no expectation that you will need any extra of these unless you have severe vomiting. Always report severe or ongoing vomiting. It is not normal after band placement. If it is happening, something is wrong. The band may be too tight, there may be a slip or prolapse, or you may be eating wrongly. It is essential that it be corrected.

Calcium is important for growth and maintenance of healthy bones. The recommended intake is 1000 mg per day. You should be able to achieve that level with the recommended food intake. Good sources include dairy products, fish, tofu and nuts. The allowed 500 mL of low-fat milk provides 650 mg alone. We have measured the bone density of people who have had the LAP-BAND™ over several years and have not been able to show any suggestion of osteoporosis developing. Nevertheless, we recommend you select a vitamin/mineral supplement containing calcium as a further guarantee.

Iron can be low, especially in menstruating women. With a low intake of iron expected on a typical post-band volume of food and little red meat, we need to watch the iron levels closely and provide supplemental iron as necessary. Good follow-up and an annual blood check should be sufficient to guard against developing iron-deficiency anemia. Good food sources of iron include red meat, spinach, beans and chicken.

There is not normally a need for supplements of magnesium, phosphorus, zinc or the trace minerals.

The vitamin/mineral preparations come in different forms and you should try a range to find the one that suits you best. We would like you to take one per day and you are not going to comply with this if the preparation is unpleasant. Generally, the tablets are large and some people will have trouble swallowing them or getting them through the area of the band. You can find it easier to buy dissolvable, liquid, chewable or spray forms.

PROCESSED FOODS VERSUS FRESH FOODS

Always eat fresh food if possible. Processed foods, foods that have undergone some manufacturing process, are not intrinsically bad. Some vitamins might be lost in the processing but the major food components remain intact. However, the manufacturers of processed foods do include all sorts of additives in them, such as salt, sugar and trans-fatty acids. These additives do not contribute usefully to the nutritional value of the food and could be undesirable. If you use processed foods, carefully check the contents on the package. It is very useful to develop the habit of reading the labels on processed foods. Seek to understand what is in the food. Become familiar with the codes for simple sugars. Look at the amount of fats. Are trans-fatty acids present? The less the better. How much protein is present? The more the better.

SO WHAT GOES INTO THE HALF A GLASS?

As we contemplate the half a glass of food for each meal, always consider the protein-containing food first. Place enough of the protein-rich food on the plate to fill at least half of our symbolic glass. Next add vegetables. Vegetables are great "fillers." They are among the least calorie-dense of all foods. They take up a lot of space but contain few calories. And they add roughage. You can make a generous allowance for the air spaces and water content of the vegetables. Fruit are a reasonable substitute for vegetables on occasions, but remember that they have a higher content of simple sugars. Starchy foods come in last, for whatever space, if any, is left.

Be sure all the food is high quality, tasty and interesting.

FLUID INTAKE AFTER THE LAP-BAND™

Adequate fluid intake is always important. Fortunately, our thirst centers in the brain know that and tell us clearly when we need to drink. We therefore do not instruct you to drink a set amount of water per day. We leave it to you and your thirst center to determine the volume you need to take. Remember that there is also a considerable volume of water in food and so our total fluid intake per day is more than what we drink. Our need for additional fluid varies quite a lot on different days. If you are having a quiet day at home in the winter you will need much less fluid than a busy

outdoor day in summer. Let your sense of thirst tell you. But do listen to it and drink when thirsty.

Please try to stay with zero-calorie liquids—water, mineral water, tea or coffee (no added sugar please)—and zero-calorie soft drinks. We set no limit on how much of these you drink.

The sugar-containing soft drinks are absolutely forbidden. Fruit juices are not allowed. They are also high in sugar, low in valuable nutrients and give no feeling of fullness or satiation.

Soup is discouraged, but the thicker the soup, the less unhappy we are. An occasional serve of soup is not going to be a problem. The danger with soup is that you will not get that feeling of fullness or satiation and therefore tend to take too much at each meal. However, a thick lentil or vegetable soup may well be just as effective in giving that satisfied feeling as a meal of soft foods well chewed.

Alcohol is a difficult one. Initially, we advised our patients not to take alcohol because it was a calorie-containing liquid. Also, it is relatively calorie-dense—7 calories (30 kJ) per gram, which is much more than carbohydrates or proteins, which provide 4 calories (20 kJ) per gram, and closer to fat at 9 calories (40 kJ) per gram. However, many of our patients did take alcohol in spite of our guidance and so we did a study to see if they lost less weight because they were "breaking the law." To our surprise, we found that, within a modest alcohol intake range, the more they had, the better the weight loss. Most were drinking wine with meals, so we cannot be sure about beer or spirits. Modest alcohol intake has a number of established health benefits, such as reduction in the risk of heart disease and strokes and better control of diabetes. Since our study, we have acknowledged a further benefit of a modest alcohol intake on health and have allowed up to seven standard drinks per week. As our patients were generally drinking Australian wine with the evening meal, we know a glass of fine Australian cabernet or shiraz with dinner is good for you.

Bon appétit.

EXERCISE AND ACTIVITY AFTER THE LAP-BAND™

KEY POINTS

- Increasing exercise and your general levels of activity is essential for optimal outcome with the **LAP-BAND™**.

- Ensure you do at least 30 minutes of exercise per day, but aim for 1 hour per day.

- Walking energetically is the commonest and perhaps the best form of exercise.

- If the back, hips or knees are wearing out, think about water aerobics, swimming or an exercise bike.

- Be active all day. Use a pedometer to encourage you to achieve a new "personal best" often.

CHAPTER 8

WHY YOU SHOULD INCREASE YOUR ACTIVITY LEVEL

Your weight loss will depend on the amount of food you eat and the amount of exercise and activity you undertake. The more energy you burn up, the thinner you will be.

The LAP-BAND™ works primarily by facilitating a reduced food intake. As you start to lose weight, it becomes easier to be active. This activity increases the weight loss, which then allows you to be even more active. The more you take advantage of that, the better weight loss you will have, the healthier you will be and the better you will feel. Your weight spirals down through the combination of less eating and more activity.

Conversely, if you cannot or do not increase your activity, you will lose less weight. Someone with extensive arthritis, for example, may not be able to increase activity very much and should not expect to have as good a weight loss as a result.

We will be encouraging you to become as active as possible. It is not only good for your weight loss, it also helps your health in general and it improves your feeling of well-being, confidence and self-esteem. We suggest you think about activity in two ways—as formal planned exercise and as the activities in your normal daily living.

EXERCISE

Many of our patients have never undertaken any exercise in their life. Others had been top athletes when they were younger and have suffered the middle-aged spread. Some will have made a major achievement by spending 30 minutes a day in gentle walking. Others will become true athletes and take up competitive sports. We want each of you to make a commitment to do the best you can. You must do something every day. Unless physically restricted by a health problem, you should seek to accumulate a total of at least 200 minutes each week in exercise.

The LAP-BAND™ does not make it easier for you to exercise, but the weight loss does. Even a few pounds of weight loss will help make you fitter, lighter and more able to become active.

This will make it easier for you to make the commitment—the commitment to start exercising, the commitment to continue to build your exercise program and the commitment to continue it on a daily basis permanently. We can advise and encourage you but we cannot do it for you. It is going to be up to you.

If you make this commitment and maintain a good exercise program, the benefits are extraordinary.

Weight loss is the benefit of particular interest to us in this situation but there are many others. Most importantly, exercise will improve your health and you are likely to live longer. Diseases such as diabetes, hypertension and abnormal fat levels in the blood are improved sharply. Developing potentially fatal diseases such as heart attacks and stroke becomes less likely. It has been estimated that, for every mile (1.6 km) you walk, you increase your lifespan by 30 minutes. The processes of aging are slowed, with the heart continuing good function, the lungs better maintaining their ability to take up oxygen, and the bones remaining strong. Lapses of memory are fewer, sleep is improved and depression is less likely. Exercising will give you a sense of well-being and health that will improve your quality of life. You will think more clearly, and work with more energy and stamina.

There are many different forms of exercise and it is worth identifying which exercises best enable you to achieve the optimal results. In general, we want you to put most effort into doing those exercises that go under the descriptors of "aerobic" or "cardio." The other forms are strength and flexibility exercises. The aerobic exercises are those that use the large muscle groups continuously for prolonged periods. Vigorous walking is perhaps the best example. Other types of aerobic exercise are bike riding, swimming and jogging. If you go to the gym, do those activities that involve low-to-moderate effort but which are repetitive, going on for several minutes.

You could do a "strength" program using heavy weights and few repetitions to gain power and body shaping. However, this is not what we are after. The central feature of the aerobic exercises is that they use most of the major muscle groups in the body, in a way that pushes up your heart rate and gets you breathing more quickly and deeply.

We want you to try to exercise each day. Make it a part of your life, plan for it, look forward to it and enjoy it. If you are doing something that you do not like, you will find excuses to miss it, and soon it is no more. Find the activities that you enjoy. Create some variety. Encourage others to exercise with you. There are few things more powerful in keeping you on your program than the commitment to meet a friend for the activity. Personal trainers are excellent in optimizing your program and providing the stimulus to keep you at it.

You should seek to do at least 200 minutes of exercise each week. Ideally, this would be achieved by doing 30 minutes each day of the week. If your other commitments do not allow for daily exercise, you can exercise on three weekdays and make up the difference on the weekend.

It is not necessary to do the 30 minutes in one block. It is equally effective if the exercise is divided into two blocks of 15 minutes or even three blocks of 10 minutes. Surely there are few of us so busy that we cannot squeeze in three 10-minute blocks of exercise each day. Just walking up 20 flights of stairs in your office building would do it. Walking 1 mile (1.6 km) down the street would do it. Riding your exercise bike for 10 minutes would do it. Just do it.

The most common exercise and one of the best is walking. For those who haven't exercised before, it is certainly the best starting point. Some of you will be limited in your ability to exercise because of health problems. Osteoarthritis involving the hips, knees or feet is a common example, but there are many others. If you are disabled with arthritis, the effort for you to walk once around the house may be equal to the effort

for a healthy person to walk for 30 minutes. As long as you make the effort, you use up energy and you help your weight loss. Do the best you can.

For those who are not physically limited by diseases such as osteoarthritis, we would be looking for you to do a minimum of 30 minutes of walking each day. Ideally, you will build up to 1 hour per day. If walking is your preferred activity, it should be a brisk walk, enough to get your pulse rate up and your breathing going. If you are doing it with a friend, it is not a stroll and a chat. It is stepping out, and conversation should be a little difficult. Make a note of how far you go and how long you take and try to improve progressively. There is no upper limit on exercise.

All forms of exercise are allowed.

There is no exercise that is excluded because of the band. You cannot hurt or move the band by exercise. The access port is under the skin and it can be tender in that region. Getting bumped there may be uncomfortable. But you cannot hurt the port itself. It is far too robust. The band itself is totally remote from any possible point of contact and cannot be damaged by any physical activity. Sometimes, when you are joining a gym and you tell them you have a LAP-BAND™, the staff may be unsure of the limits placed by the band. They may even request a physician's certificate to guide them about the implications.

Please reassure them. Show them this page of the book. There is nothing that can happen to the band or the port. There is no need for a certificate. Just get going.

Look for variety in what you do. Keep it interesting. Do some of those activities that you have missed because of your weight problem—a hike in the local national park, a bike ride, kicking the football with the kids, swimming or surfing at your local beach, horse riding. Table 8.1 provides just a sample of the options. Try them all and add to the list. Remember that these activities are good in every way—good for the effectiveness of the band, good for your health, good for your quality of life and good fun. These include the things you missed out on because of your weight. Go for them now.

TABLE 8.1 THE ACTIVITIES OPTIONS

Walking, jogging, running	Riding horses
Bike riding —road bike	Rowing, canoeing, kayaking
—mountain bike	Skiing —downhill
—exercise bike	—cross-country
Bushwalking/hiking	Football —Australian Rules
Aerobics —at the gym or at home	—Rugby
—water aerobics	—American football
Stretching exercises	—soccer
Dancing —any style	Basketball, netball, volleyball
—no style	Hockey
Swimming	Baseball, softball
Tennis, squash, racketball,	Roller-blading, roller-skating,
table tennis	ice-skating
Golf (no carts please)	

If you are limited in your activities by pain in the back, hips, knees or feet, look to the non–weight bearing exercises. Water aerobics and swimming are excellent activities. Riding an exercise bike might be possible if walking is difficult.

PERSONAL TRAINER

If you can afford it, a personal trainer is invaluable, especially as you get started. The personal trainer should be able to evaluate your particular abilities, needs and interests. He or she can then establish reasonable goals, design a program of exercise that is optimal for you to reach those goals, and guide you in correct technique. Most importantly, the personal trainer motivates you to keep reaching your goals. However, a word of warning—some personal trainers move into dietary advice and recommend five or six meals a day "to get your metabolism going." Don't listen to that. It may have some validity for an Olympic athlete in training. It is not correct for a person with a gastric band.

THE EXCUSES FOR NOT EXERCISING

There are many things that seem to get in the way of an exercise program. You miss your planned activities for what you feel are perfectly good reasons. We hear them all the time. After placement of the LAP-BAND™ a number of excuses are disallowed, forbidden, not recognized, not permitted. All of the following excuses are on the disallowed list:

• I had the flu.
• I just didn't have time.
• I was on holidays.
• I was overseas.
• My mother/husband/kids were sick.
• I am not thin enough yet.
• I can't afford to go to the gym.
• I have no one to look after the kids.
• I work all day every day.
• And any other not listed.

No excuse is allowed. You must exercise. It must be given priority. Picture the cartoon of the doctor asking his busy executive patient: "Which fits into your busy schedule better—exercising 1 hour a day or being dead 24 hours a day?"

ACTIVITIES OF DAILY LIVING

Formal exercises, such as the ones we have listed in Table 8.1, are really only a small part of the energy we use each day in being active. Most of our energy is used in the simple activities of daily living.

Activities of daily living include walking around the house, going to work or shopping—just doing the things we need to do. You can increase your energy use quite a lot by increasing these activities.

Get up earlier and keep active through the day. Regard sitting down as a wasted opportunity. Be standing rather than sitting. Be walking rather than standing. Be outside rather than inside.

Look for excuses to be more active. Park the car at the back corner of the car park of the shopping center, rather than waiting for a spot near the entrance. Or better, leave the car at home and walk to the shops. Use the stairs, not the escalator. Get involved in activities in the community. Do things with the family. Take up

a sport. Become a tourist in your own community by visiting and revisiting all the interesting places.

Use temperature to help. We use a lot of energy just keeping our body temperature within its normal range. In an air-conditioned environment of about 70°F (21°C), you will be using the least amount of energy for temperature control. If the temperature is higher or lower than 70°F (21°C), you will use energy to maintain your body temperature. Leave the air conditioner or heating off. Be outside as much as possible where the temperature is whatever nature has determined. You are much more likely to be active when you are outside. We tend to keep moving, doing things, when outside, whereas we tend to sit when inside.

As your weight comes down, your capacity to do things becomes much greater, partly because you have less weight to carry, partly because of improved health and partly because of the psychological feeling of relief that a problem that has been the bane of your life has disappeared. Use this increased enthusiasm for activity to do all the things that need to be done, and then look for more.

A pedometer is one way of getting feedback on how active you are. The pedometer is meant to encourage you to be active. Use it as a stimulus to show that you are improving. Make sure that today you do more than yesterday. Make sure that this week you are more active than last week. You should seek to exceed 10,000 steps per day. Always be trying to achieve a new personal best.

PATIENT ANECDOTE
DAN FORD

I played sports growing up and through high school. My activities kept me in shape and my weight down. When I got out of school I got out of sports. Time, family and other priorities took over my life. Although I longed for the teamwork, camaraderie and, more importantly, the physical fitness involved with sports, my weight would not allow me to participate at the level I wanted to. I have tried all the fad diets. Some with little or no success and others with marked success until I could no longer either afford them or continue to structure my life around diets that did not allow me to participate with my family. Food is life. Almost everything we do has food associated with it. The fad diets that did work only brought more guilt when the weight came back and with it disappointment and failure, which always seemed to go hand in hand with dieting.

Then I learned about the LAP-BAND™. I had trouble at first believing that with the band the weight would not come back, that it was not a diet but a tool, and that I was in total control of my weight loss. Even better than that, once I hit my goal the band would be there to help me maintain that weight for the rest of my life. As a bonus, all the sports and family activities I had missed out on for over 20 years would be within my reach.

I had my surgery May 12, 2005. The surgery went perfectly and I actually went into work the following day to check on appointments and messages. I had no pain whatsoever. Although my results are not typical, I hit my goal within 5 months! Down 170 lb (77 kg)! A world of opportunities has reopened for me. There is nothing I can't do. More importantly, there is nothing I can't experience with my children. All the things I stayed away from I can now do, whether it's playing softball with my daughter or ice-skating with my son, who plays ice hockey. The LAP-BAND™ has given me my life back. It had been so long I had almost forgotten.

ADJUSTING THE LAP-BAND™

CHAPTER 9

KEY POINTS

- The adjustability of the LAP-BAND™ is its most important feature. We should use it skillfully, wisely and with enthusiasm.

- We are seeking a state of satiety, of not being hungry, of not being interested in food, of being in the "green zone." Work with us.

- Too little fluid in the band is wasting the opportunity. Too much fluid is harming the process.

- There will always be a need for some fine adjustment. Therefore, there is always a need for follow-up consultations.

185

ADJUSTABILITY OF THE LAP-BAND™

Without doubt, the best feature of the LAP-BAND™ is its adjustability. Optimal adjustment of the band is the key to effective weight loss.

You need to understand this process to get the best results.

When we place the band during the operation, all the free space within it is filled with a basal amount of saline fluid. For the LAP-BAND™ AP series this is usually 3 mL. Depending on how tight it appears to be at operation, your surgeon may increase or decrease this amount. This then becomes your starting volume. We want you to get over the operation without having to cope with a very tight band at the same time. In particular, we want to avoid you having any difficulties with swallowing fluid or food or having any vomiting early after placement of the band. The initial 4-week period after operation is set aside for the band to settle into position and for the surrounding tissues to become firm so that there is less chance of the band moving at a later time.

THE FIRST 4 WEEKS

We generally start to add saline to the band about 4 weeks after placement. During the first 4 weeks you are not going to be feeling very hungry and you will be losing weight. In particular, it is usual for you to feel no hunger or interest in food during the first week and most of the weight loss occurs in that time. During the next 3 weeks the feeling of hunger and interest in food returns and the weight loss slows or stops.

Remember that feeling of lack of hunger and lack of interest in food during the first week. That is the sense of satiety that we will be seeking to reproduce. We will be looking to return you to that state of satiety by adjusting the band. If you remember it well, you can guide us. You can tell us if you are not back to that point, or that you recognize that you have returned to the same level of satiety as you felt that first week.

Typically, by the end of that 4-week period, you will notice that you are eating too easily, that you can eat larger amounts of food than you thought you should be eating and you may also be getting hungry between meals. This is normal. These are the signals that you need fluid added. We will normally start this at 4 weeks. The amount of fluid we add depends on a number of factors and is really a medical decision. It will depend on the type of band you have, the amount of hunger or satiety you have experienced during the 4 weeks, the weight loss that has occurred and the approach to adjustment used. Normally, for the LAP-BAND™ AP series, we will confirm that the baseline amount is present (commonly 3 mL) and then add between 1.0 mL and 1.5 mL to give a total volume of 4.0 mL to 4.5 mL.

It is worth being aware of the approximate amount of fluid in the band, but please do not focus on this too much. There is nothing magical about any particular volume and there is no reason to believe that the volume your friend has is any better than what you have. The key to the adjustments is to achieve the feeling of satiety, of non-hunger, of disinterest in food. Whatever volume of fluid is needed to achieve this is the correct volume. Increasing the volume beyond this is likely to harm, not help. Too much fluid and you will be in what we call the "red zone" (see inside back cover).

In the LAP-BAND™ world on the Internet, a concept of "the fill" has built up in discussions on blogs and chat rooms, as if it were the be-all and end-all. It is not. "Fill" is a four-letter word beginning with "F" and I don't want you to ever say it. Correct adjustment is so much more than going to a "fill center" and getting a "fill." It is a real clinical consultation. It involves sitting down with someone knowledgeable and experienced, usually a physician or nurse practitioner, talking about your eating pattern, talking about any difficulties, reviewing for symptoms that something might not be quite right, looking at the weight loss, giving advice about eating, exercise and activity and, after all of that, maybe making an adjustment. The adjustment is a part of the clinical consultation; it is not a procedure independent of clinical assessment.

With the addition of fluid we are looking to achieve two effects—satiety or the feeling of not being hungry even when you haven't been eating, and satiation, the feeling of being satisfied after eating. The effectiveness of the band will vary depending on whether we are near to the optimal setting for the band or not. Whether you feel a sense of satiety and satiation helps us know if we need to add more fluid at each visit or whether we are close to the optimal setting. It is very important that you understand these effects. If you do, you are able to work with the band to get the best result and you can guide us in achieving a correct balance for you.

1 SATIETY

The first effect of adding fluid is that you will feel less hungry.

You acquire a feeling of satiety, which is another way of saying that you are not hungry or have no appetite for food.

This is the more important of the two effects and the principal reason why the band works so well. For many of our patients, it will be the first time in their life that they can remember not feeling hungry. They are not thinking about food. They are not looking to eat and they can go for many hours without eating because they simply don't have any interest in food.

This feeling of satiety will enable you to stick to the rule of not having more than three meals per day. We don't mind if you have fewer than three meals per day, but we do not want you to have more than three. Not even a cookie or a piece of fruit. If, after an adjustment, you find that you are still looking for a snack between meals or even feeling hungry, tell us and we can add more fluid. This is one of the important markers to us that you need more fluid.

2 SATIATION

The second effect of adjustment is to give you a feeling that you have eaten enough after taking only a small amount of food.

This is called satiation, a sense of being satisfied by the amount of food that you have eaten.

If the amount of fluid added is optimal, you will eat only a small amount and be comfortable. We want you to stop eating at that point. Do not go on and eat until you feel full. By then you will have eaten too much. Eat just enough to take away any feeling of hunger and then stop.

To achieve satiation, you must eat slowly. The signals from the stomach to the brain to tell you that you have eaten enough pass only slowly. How often do you recall feeling like an extra serve of some nice food, eating it, and then, 20 minutes later, regretting that you ate the extra bit as you now feel too full? It takes 10 to 15 minutes for the feeling of satiation to become clear. We don't want you ever to get that full feeling. For a start, it means you are eating too much and if you keep doing it you will stretch the new "mini" stomach, which will get larger as a consequence and then we may have a problem. And you will not be losing the weight that we both want you to lose. That is two bad outcomes from eating too much, from eating to fullness rather than to the point of not being hungry.

The best strategy to enable you to eat only just enough food and to recognize the sense of satiation is to always use a small plate, put a small amount of food on the plate, eat slowly and always try to leave some. Let's call this the "angels' share." Try not to eat everything on the plate. Get in the habit of throwing out food. Leave some for the angels. If you haven't left some food on the plate, you may need a further adjustment. It is especially important to eat slowly. Even though the amount of food is small, stretch each meal out to 20 minutes. Play around with your food. Push it around the plate. Stop after each bite and consider whether you need another one. If you feel that you no longer need any more food, stop and discard what is left. If you are still feeling you need more, take another bite and then reconsider.

Chew well; don't gulp the food down. The two worst eating practices you could have are to eat too quickly and to eat too much volume. These will stretch that new "mini" stomach and, if you do it repeatedly, eventually the stomach above the band will stretch and this may need fixing surgically.

You will be amazed at how little you need to eat and how little you will feel like eating. As a community we all overeat. Almost everyone eats too much, but some are fortunate to be able to burn off the excess energy and therefore not put on extra weight. However, more and more of us are storing some of the extra food as fat and that is why about two-thirds of the adult population are now either overweight or obese.

Once you have the band, those around you, especially your family, will notice how little you are eating and may worry that you should eat more. They can sabotage your best efforts through this misunderstanding. You must resist any pressure to eat more than we recommend. The pressure may come from your family, your friends, your work colleagues and even some of the health professionals that you may see. Learn to recognize what is happening and put up your guard against it. Be polite but firm. Don't be seduced. They may have only good intentions. They may have bad intentions and, through envy or whatever reason, are truly trying to sabotage your efforts. Whatever, stick to the rules.

As described in Chapter 7, you should eat the amount of food you can get into half a glass. If you are eating or wanting to eat more than that, we need to consider adding more fluid to the band. Use the image of the amount of food you can get into half a glass as you serve yourself. Use a small plate and a small spoon or fork. Serve yourself away from the table. Do not have the food served at the table. It is too easy and tempting to have a bit more. Take your small serve to the table, eat it slowly, push it around, play with it, take very small bites and leave some for the angels.

Think of strategies that help you eat slowly. Talk with your family. Read at least one page of a book or a newspaper article between bites. Knit. Watch television. Do anything that helps you to eat slowly, to stretch the meal out to 20 minutes. And always think "20–20–20, wait a minute" (page 153).

HOW TO GET TO KNOW AND LOVE THE "GREEN ZONE"

The "green zone" is a concept developed within our group to explain visually where we are trying to get to with our adjustments. It is well worthwhile studying the figure on the inside back cover and understanding it. You can then place yourself somewhere in or between the zones. Your view of where you are helps us decide about adding or removing fluid from the band. We have put the "green zone" figure on the inside back cover so that you can find it easily. It is a key concept in the adjustment process. Please get to know it, to understand it, and to love it. Refer to it frequently and always try to estimate where you are along the scale.

Let's discuss what the figure illustrates.

1   **The yellow zone**. You are in the yellow zone if you have not had enough fluid added to the band. There is too much space within the band for food to pass through and too little effect of causing satiety and satiation. The band is not compressing the stomach enough to give a background of satiety and the esophagus is squeezing the food through easily. The nerve endings (the IGLEs) are probably not being stimulated enough. You will still get hungry and look for food between meals (lack of satiety). You will be inclined to eat too much at a meal and not leave

any for the angels (lack of satiation). You will be having no weight loss or it may not be as rapid as we would like. This is common during the first few weeks after the placement of the band. Our main aim with the initial series of adjustments is to get you out of the yellow zone and into the green zone.

2 **The green zone**. This is the target zone. This is where we want you to be. In the green zone you are not hungry. Food is not of much interest and you spend little time thinking about food, or meals, or what you will have for dinner, or what you will buy at the supermarket. You have simply lost interest. When you do eat, you will notice that you do not feel like eating much. You will feel comfortable and not hungry after a small amount of food. You should be able to eat a fairly broad range of food, but some food like red meat, fresh bread and rice can be difficult. You can place a small amount of food on a plate, maybe equal to the amount of food you could compress into half a glass, and you will be happy to leave some. Once you have finished a meal you are not interested in eating anything until the next mealtime. Your weight should be dropping by about 2 lb (1 kg) or more per week early after the operation and about 1 lb (0.5 kg) per week after 6 months or so.

3 **The red zone**. You go into the red zone if we make the band too tight or if there is something wrong

with its position that causes an obstruction. Eating solid food becomes more difficult. You prefer softer or liquid food. The range of food that you can eat becomes limited. Many good foods won't stay down. Food will "stick" at the lower part of the esophagus. You feel a tightness at the lower chest. You may vomit or need to go to the bathroom and bring up what seems to be stuck. Soft slippery food like chocolate and ice cream become preferred. They can slide down, whereas good food cannot. We call this "maladaptive eating." It does not occur because you are evil and not cooperating and cannot follow a simple, clear set of rules. It occurs because the band is too tight. If the band is too tight, people can actually put on weight because they are eating the wrong food. We can take out some fluid and the weight loss gets going again. This may seem curious but it is typical of what happens when people have moved into the red zone. Stay out of that area or, if you think you may have slipped into it, talk to us and we can see if some fluid needs to be removed.

Note that more fluid in the band is not necessarily better. It is common to meet patients with the LAP-BAND™ who believe that the more fluid we add to the band, the better the weight loss. You can see discussion of this in chat rooms on the Internet and you see people become concerned because they have less fluid than someone else. From this discussion of the green and red zones we hope that you can see that this is not true. Too much fluid in the band can be harmful. Finding the correct setting for you and then maintaining you at that level is the main challenge of the follow-up period. It requires clinical assessment and careful clinical judgment. The final decision about making an adjustment and about how much to add is a medical one, but you are able to guide us considerably by understanding what we are trying to achieve.

THE PROCESS OF ADJUSTMENTS

People worry about the adjustments, particularly before the first one. Some of our patients have said they worried more about that first adjustment than they did about the operation. There is something about getting jabbed with a needle that just does not appeal to everyone.

Please don't worry. It is not that bad. It should be about the same as having a blood sample taken for testing. Both generally are straightforward and involve a single stab and then it's over. On occasions both can be difficult but hopefully not for you.

WHAT HAPPENS WITH AN ADJUSTMENT?

Office adjustments

We recommend doing the adjustments in the consulting room. You lie on the examination table with a pillow placed under the middle of your back. This pushes your tummy up and makes it easier for us to feel the port. Once we feel the port, we usually put a mark on the skin directly over it using a marker pen. This indicates where the needle should be placed. We put some antiseptic on the skin and, while that is working, we select the length of needle that should be able to reach the port comfortably and attach it to a syringe that is appropriate for the fluid volume of the band at that time. We pop the needle through the skin. This is usually the only bit of pain.

The needle then passes through the fat under the skin down to the surface of the port. As fat has very few nerve fibers that detect pain, this is usually pain-free. We then get you to cross your arm across your chest and lift your head up off the bunk. This causes the muscle layer to which the port is attached to become quite firm and makes it a lot easier for the needle to go through the injection plug of the port.

Once the needle is inside the port, we may draw out all of the fluid into the syringe so that we can measure the volume, making sure that it is the volume we expected, and that there is none missing. We then add that fluid back in and also add the additional fluid that we have agreed is needed. More often we simply add the fluid needed. Taking out all the fluid and then putting it all back can make the band too tight for a day or two. By just adding fluid, we can usually avoid this.

We then withdraw the needle and may place a Band-Aid over the spot. Generally the procedure takes only 2 or 3 minutes. Note that the only fluid we use is saline. It is totally harmless.

Radiological adjustments

While we almost always do the adjustments in the office, some groups prefer to do the adjustments in the radiology department. The needle is put into the port while imaging with X-rays. You then stand in front of the X-ray machine and drink some liquid barium. They watch this pass through the area of the band. Fluid is added to the port until there is only a narrow column of barium passing through. The needle is then removed.

We are not in favor of the radiological method as the costs are higher, it requires much more of your time and ours, and you will get quite a dose of radiation every time you have an adjustment. If there is any possibility that you may be pregnant, make sure you mention that before agreeing to a radiological adjustment. We see the adjustment as just one part of the clinical consultation. The office model lends itself to that, whereas adjustments in radiology tend to be just a "fill" and any clinical discussions and assessments generally will have to occur elsewhere. We have no data to suggest that there is any better or worse outcome with either method. We therefore prefer to keep it simple and safe.

AFTER THE ADJUSTMENT

We make the adjustments in a stepwise fashion over many weeks, seeking slowly but progressively to get to the correct setting. It is simply not possible to go directly to the final volume. You would certainly be blocked off or at least in the red zone. After each adjustment, there is an adaptation, a settling in, a molding of the band and the stomach. After an adjustment, typically you will feel quite tight in the area for 2 or 3 days and then you will notice it gets easier.

You may have trouble taking solid food and have to go back to soft food or even liquids for these 2 or 3 days. We don't insist that you do that. We are happy to leave it to you to decide. If you are struggling with solid food, go back to the softer food. If you cannot cope with the softer food, go back to liquids only. If you cannot cope with liquids, come back to the clinic to have some of the fluid removed. We must have added too much too quickly. On most occasions you will notice a significant difference after an adjustment but will still cope with solid food. After 2 or 3 days you will find it a little easier but hopefully still significant and you will be eating less than before the adjustment.

MAKING THE DECISION TO ADJUST

This is very much a joint decision. You will know if you are still hungry, if you are eating too easily and maybe too big a volume, and you will sense that you are not losing weight fast enough. We will be asking you about hunger, appetite, volume and type of food, and presence of symptoms such as vomiting or heartburn, which could indicate that you are in the yellow or red zones rather than the green zone. We will measure your weight and look at how much you have lost since the last visit. We will also be looking at your overall rate of weight loss.

It can happen that you do not lose much weight over a 2- or even 4-week period yet we are happy with your overall progress because you had lost more weight than expected at an earlier time and you are on track to achieving our target for weight loss. There can be fluctuations in the rate of weight loss at times for poorly defined reasons. If your overall weight loss is fine, we are not necessarily going to react to any single period of slow weight loss. We see your progress toward our targets very readily on LapBase, our computer record of your baseline and follow-up details, and can show you whether you are on track to your target or not. This is a great help in deciding whether you need further adjustments and of reassuring you after a slow month. It also shows clearly if we are going too slowly, in which case we will review your eating and exercise patterns, and consider adding more fluid to the band.

From the first adjustment at 4 weeks, visits should occur at 2-weekly intervals until you feel that you are in the green zone. This may require two to four more

visits. After each adjustment you are likely to feel an exaggerated effect for the first 2 to 3 days before settling into a new level of satiety and restriction. By the end of the week after an adjustment you are usually able to recognize whether you are sufficiently restricted. We could arrange to see you and do further adjustment at that time but usually we prefer to wait an extra week to allow you to be sure of the effects on appetite and eating and to allow us enough time to check your weight loss over a longer period.

As we get nearer to the green zone we can stretch out the interval between visits to 4 weeks, 6 weeks, 3 months and eventually to 6 months. We do not want to ever have a gap of more than 6 months between visits. Remember the eighth of our golden rules is "Always keep in contact." You must always be coming back for check-ups, with 6 months the longest duration between check-ups that we would like to happen. At all visits, doing adjustments is just one of the tasks we want to do. We also want to discuss your eating practices and your exercise program. We want to check whether you are taking supplements of vitamins and minerals. We want to inquire about symptoms that could indicate that the band is too tight or misplaced, and we want to be checking on the activity of your other health problems and their treatments. Please do not see these visits as solely for "a fill." They should always be proper medical consultations and adding fluid to the band is just one of many important tasks to be completed.

Nevertheless, keeping the volume of fluid in the band is one of the most important tasks and it will remain so even years after the band has been placed. You should always expect that the need for further adjustments will

be ongoing, for two reasons. Firstly, there is a continuing process of adaptation or molding of the band and
the stomach. What was tight enough at one time may
be too loose 6 months later. Secondly, there is a slight
loss of fluid from the band over time. If you had 7.0
mL placed at an adjustment, you could expect that 6
months later that volume may have dropped to 6.7 mL.
That small loss of fluid is enough to lead to overeating.
If you were unaware of this small fluid loss, you may
think that you are failing and blame yourself. In reality,
you just need a top-up. That would get you back into
the green zone.

WEIGHT LOSS AFTER THE LAP-BAND™

KEY POINTS

- Weight loss is the first, and the most important, measure of the effect of the LAP-BAND™.

- We aim to have everyone lose two-thirds of their excess weight.

- Weight loss should happen slowly, stretching out for 1 to 3 years after placement of the LAP-BAND™.

- Failure to lose enough weight will occur if the adjustments are not correct or you are not following the eating and exercise rules, or the follow-up visits are not frequent enough.

CHAPTER 10

QUESTIONS ABOUT WEIGHT LOSS

The primary reason for having the LAP-BAND™ placed is to lose weight. Through weight loss, there should be an improvement in your physical and mental health, you should have a better quality of life and you can expect to live longer.

Questions foremost in your mind as you anticipate the benefits of the LAP-BAND™ probably are:

- How much weight will I lose?
- How quickly will I lose it?
- Could I fail to lose enough weight?
- What must I do to get the best weight loss?

Let us discuss each of these questions in turn.

HOW MUCH WEIGHT WILL I LOSE?

On average, people will lose between 50% and 66% of their excess weight.

Our patients typically have 125 lb (57 kg) of excess weight. The excess weight is fat. We both want you to lose as much of the fat as possible. Not all of it, as we do need some fat, but two-thirds of it would be a very good outcome in the medium term and, on average, our thousands of patients have lost between a half and two-thirds of it. If you are the "typical" person, you should lose between 60 and 84 lb (27 and 40 kg) in weight.

If your starting weight is lower, that is, if you have less excess weight, you will lose fewer pounds (kilograms) but probably a greater percentage of your excess weight. If you are bigger, that is, if you have more excess weight, you are likely to lose more pounds (kilograms) of weight but a lower percentage of your excess weight, simply because there is so much more to lose.

As an example, let us compare the outcomes for some-one weighing 600 lb (272 kg), who has 450 lb (204 kg) of excess weight, with someone who is 220 lb (100 kg) and has 66 lb (20 kg) of excess weight. If the first person lost 225 lb (102 kg), they would have lost 50% of the excess weight, whereas the second person could lose just 33 lb (15 kg) and would also have lost 50% of excess weight. You could regard both outcomes as about equal and yet the numbers are quite different. When we indicate a particular weight is a realistic target, we are taking into consideration your initial weight.

It is important to understand how we calculate your excess weight and how we set the targets for weight loss. It is also important for you to realize and accept that we are not aiming to have you lose all of your excess weight. We are aiming to improve your health and your likelihood of living a full length of life, without the physi-cal and psychosocial disabilities that obesity causes.

We regard the normal weight for the population as being a BMI of between 18.5 and 25. If you have a BMI of 25, you are at the upper limit of normal. Any weight above that is excess to normal. We therefore calculate the weight you would have to be to have a BMI of 25 and subtract that value from your current weight. The difference is the excess weight. As you lose some of that excess weight we often describe this as a percentage, using the term "percentage of excess weight lost." For instance, if your excess weight is 130 lb (60 kg) at the time of band placement and you have lost 65 lb (30 kg), you would have lost 50% of your excess weight.

We set several targets for the amount of weight reduction we would like each person to achieve.

These targets are calculated automatically on LapBase, the computer database that we have developed to help us follow your progress. The first target is to have you lose two-thirds of your excess weight. We set this target when we were beginning to use the LAP-BAND™ back in the early 1990s. We now have measures on several thousand patients and we know that, while many do lose two-thirds or 66% of their excess weight, overall, we are not able to achieve that target for all patients. On average, our patients are losing between 50% and 66% of their excess weight. This is the reality. Still, it doesn't hurt to have a target that is a little ahead of your normal reach. That way we keep working with you to get to that target.

If you do succeed in losing two-thirds of your excess weight, the next target we set on LapBase is to have you reach a BMI of 27. We have selected this target because, although you are still in the overweight category (BMI 25–30), anyone with a BMI below 27 is generally seen to be free of the risks of the disease of obesity and the risk of premature death. An exception to this is those who have type 2 diabetes, who are better off with as low a weight as they can achieve. For the rest, a BMI of 27 puts you into a medically safe area.

The final target we set on LapBase is for you to reach a BMI of 25. You are now of normal weight. You have lost 100% of your excess weight. This is a very fine achievement, of which you should be proud. However, for most people, there is no clear health benefit in that final burst of weight loss. It tends to be a cosmetic benefit rather than a medical one—you look great but you may not be any healthier. Very few will reach this target and it is age-related. Our teenagers can do it, but if you are over 40 you are less likely to. Nevertheless, if you can achieve it, we are delighted for you. If you happen to have type 2 diabetes, it is also a very real health benefit for you.

All of these targets are automatically available for you on LapBase and we are keen to share them with you. If you do not know where you are going, you are not going to know if and when you get there. However, we must be realistic and we must acknowledge the very important benefits of even a small weight loss.

On average, the weight loss will be between 50% and 66% of excess weight. Many people will lose more and many will lose less. It is well established that even losing 25% of excess weight leads to an improvement in health and quality of life. We would be disappointed if this was all we achieved, but it can happen and sometimes we are forced to accept limited benefits. As a general rule, we regard a weight loss of less than 25% of excess weight as being unsatisfactory and for these people we implement our "intensive care pathway" to get them to a better level. Losing between 25% and 50% of excess weight is acceptable and worthwhile, but rather ordinary and we would be constantly looking for improvement on this loss. Any weight loss of more the 50% of excess weight is good. It provides major health advantages, a longer life and a better quality of life. We will be pushing you steadily until you have achieved at least that amount.

HOW QUICKLY WILL I LOSE IT?

We prefer a steady progression of gentle weight loss for between 18 months and 3 years.

We all seek instant gratification. We want what we want immediately, if not sooner. Not so with the LAP-BAND™. A great strength of the LAP-BAND™ compared to early forms of weight-loss surgery, such as stomach stapling, is that the weight loss happens in a sensible way.

We have control. The band is adjustable. We set the effect of satiety through adjusting the band. We tailor that setting to achieve a steady progression of weight loss, not a sudden drop.

With weight loss surgery in the past, such as gastric bypass and other forms of stomach stapling, we had no control of the settings after we had finished the operation and left the operating room. What was set during the stapling procedure had to be correct forever. It had to be loose enough that the person could eat and drink in the days immediately after the procedure and yet still be an effective restriction on eating 10 years later. This is just not possible. The body changes, it adapts and what was initially quite tight becomes looser. In order to seek some long-term control on weight, the settings were often made very tight at the start, leading to very rapid weight loss during the first 6 months, with a considerable loss of muscle as well as of fat. This is not at all what we want. There was some further weight loss for up to 12 months, but generally that was all. Whatever you had lost at 12 months was about all that you were going to lose. As a result, it was often a tough first 12 months, with good weight loss but not a good quality of life, with very little food intake and plenty of vomiting. The weight then tended to remain stable for 2 or 3 more years. After that there was a slow progression of weight gain and there was not much we or you could do to stop it.

We do not seek this pattern of rapid weight loss with the LAP-BAND™. There is good evidence that rapid weight loss is unhealthy. We are seeking changes for a lifetime and we prefer to get these changes steadily in place over at least 18 months. For some people, weight loss is more rapid and, as long as there are no problems, such as vomiting or severe limitations on eating, we do not inter-fere. But we are not going to push you to achieve that by further adjusting while the weight loss is progress-ing. The adjustment is determined largely by the weight loss. If you are progressing well, with good weight loss, no negative symptoms, and you are not feeling hungry or eating too much at mealtimes, we see you as being in the green zone (see Chapter 9) and allow you to prog-ress. If, however, weight loss is slow, you are getting hungry and eating too easily, we see you as being in the yellow zone and in need of further adjustments.

The average BMI of all of our patients is approximately 45. If you are at about this level, we would expect you to lose half of your excess weight by the end of the first year and to lose two-thirds of your excess weight by 18 to 24 months. This will easily be achieved if, on average, you lose about 2.2 lb (1 kg) per week in the first 6 months after placement of the band and then an average of 1.1 lb (0.5 kg) per week over the next year.

However, these expectations are very dependent on your initial BMI. If you have a very high BMI, such as 70 or 80, you have many more pounds (kilograms) to lose and this will take longer, but the number of pounds (kilograms) lost per week will be higher. We would be expecting a weight loss of 4.4 lb (2 kg) or more per week initially, and we would expect it to take 3 years or even more to reach the target of losing two-thirds of excess weight. If you are relatively slim, maybe a BMI of 34, you will lose fewer pounds (kilograms) per week but you should achieve that target of two-thirds of excess weight lost by 12 months or even sooner.

This is where the LapBase software helps us greatly. On the screen we can see if you are on track to these targets or if you are moving too slowly. Weight loss is never constant. Some weeks it seems easy and other weeks, even though you believe that you are following all the rules, you just don't seem to move. That happens. With LapBase, we can tell if, overall, you are on track to the targets. In general we are looking for you to lose one-third of your excess weight at 6 months and one-half at 12 months. If you are on track, we can reassure you even if it has been a slow week. If you are not, we can look for a reason and hopefully we can correct whatever is not optimal.

COULD I FAIL TO LOSE ENOUGH WEIGHT?

Of course. Nothing is perfect and, while the vast majority of the people we treat will experience a good weight loss, there are some for whom we have not achieved enough. You are not happy and we are not happy.

We will always be keen to work with you to resolve the problem. Over the years and with experience of looking after thousands of patients, we have learnt much about why some people get better results than others. We certainly don't know everything yet and we cannot be sure we can succeed with everybody but, for most of those who are not doing well, we can identify possible causes and usually we can correct them.

If we can see that you are not progressing as well as we had hoped, we move you to our "intensive care" program. This includes an analysis of all the possible causes for a poor outcome, correction of those that we can correct and an increased frequency of visits to optimize the adjustments. We would also increase the support for good eating practices and push for more exercise and increases in the activities of daily living.

WHAT MUST I DO TO GET THE BEST OUTCOME?

The best results after placement of the LAP-BAND™ will occur when there is a partnership between you and your surgeon.

The surgeon has a range of responsibilities and tasks that must be done properly and you have a range of responsibilities and tasks that you must do properly. If we both fulfill our part of the partnership, we can almost always achieve reasonable outcomes.

These roles in the partnership have been listed in Chapter 5 but we will repeat them here for your benefit.

SURGEON'S THREE COMMITMENTS

1 To place the band correctly and safely.

2 To ensure the patient is able to access good follow-up.

3 To teach the patient the rules to follow to fulfill their role.

PATIENT'S THREE COMMITMENTS

1 To follow the rules regarding eating and drinking, as discussed in Chapter 7.

2 To follow the rules regarding exercise and activity, as discussed in Chapter 8.

3 To come back for follow-up permanently with visits at least once every 6 months.

If we both fulfill our tasks optimally you will be able to achieve good weight loss, better health, and an improved quality and length of life. It is certainly worth the effort.

PATIENT ANECDOTE
REBECCA BOUTSIKOUDIS

I have tried all the diets from A to Z. I was usually able to lose some, but always gained it back the minute I went off the plan. I have always had problems with portion control. I might eat the right things, but in mega-size portions. I was a big carb eater too, so when I did the low-carb diet, it was such a drastic change that I could not stick to it.

The plans were too hard for me to stick with on any long-term basis. I became more and more isolated, uncomfortable and embarrassed about my appearance as the weight just packed on. Physically, I panted going up a flight of stairs, had no energy, was taking full-blown asthma medicine, had knee and back pain, and severe chronic heartburn. I felt like my body was falling apart and my life along with it. Although I am considered a "people person" by many, my self-esteem was very low. I was miserable. When my eating and weight were out of control, I felt like my whole life was out of control.

My father, a physician, told me about the LAP-BAND™ and encouraged me to look into it. He has seen me struggle all my life with my weight. I knew about the gastric bypass, but ruled that out as too invasive, with too many complications and the possibility of too many nutritional issues. I read about people who had to take vitamin B12 shots for the rest of their lives. I wanted something as close to natural as I could get.

I began researching the LAP-BAND™ and joined several groups so I could read about everyone's experiences—positive and negative. I basically learned that if you are ready and willing to commit to a new lifestyle, the LAP-BAND™ is for you. I was definitely ready. I liked the fact that the procedure carried minimal risk and was reversible. I also liked the fact that it was adjustable to each person's needs. This is not a "cookie cutter" operation. The principle of the LAP-BAND™ is so simple, yet so effective. Restrict the amount you can eat, but still feel full while only eating a little. The less you eat, the less calories consumed, and *voilà* ... painless weight loss.

I made the commitment and did the operation. I was scared at first that I would not succeed, but I had the right positive mental attitude. I followed the advice of my nutritionist and physicians very closely. After the weight started coming off at a steady pace I started feeling confident that I could do this—*and the band really does work, I am doing this and I am not hungry!* I knew I was in control of my eating finally, at last. It has given me the confidence to know I will not gain the weight back as I did every time before.

I lost 110 pounds (50 kg) and I have gone from a tight size 26 to a size 6 petite. I have never looked back, only forward, enjoying my new life. Physically, my back and knee pain have disappeared, my heartburn has disappeared and I am only taking one asthma medication. I can walk 2 miles (3.2 km) without thinking about it and even enjoying it now. Emotionally, I have more self-confidence and have the energy to concentrate on having a life that is not centered around food. I can center it around my family, career and friends.

I have the need to share the LAP-BAND™ with anyone I come across that is struggling with weight loss. I want to tell everyone that this is the one thing that works and keeps working. It does not go away; it does not allow you to "fall off the wagon." It is a consistent reminder that I made a decision to control my eating and live a healthy lifestyle.

I feel a sense of freedom in my new body. I live comfortably and with the confidence knowing each day I am in control.

Would I have the surgery for the LAP-BAND™ again? In a heartbeat. I wish I had taken control earlier in life. Now that I have, the world is at my doorstep!

THE EIGHT GOLDEN RULES OF EATING AND EXERCISE

1 Eat three or less small meals per day.

2 Do not eat anything between meals.

3 Eat slowly and stop when no longer hungry.

4 Focus on nutritious foods.

5 Avoid calorie-containing liquids.

6 Exercise for at least 30 minutes every day.

7 Be active throughout each day.

8 Always keep in contact with us.

We have formulated eight "golden rules" for getting the best result from the procedure. It is of vital importance that you follow these rules. The success of the procedure requires us to place the band correctly, but it equally requires that you follow these rules.

We have been tempted to call them guidelines rather than rules. They are not absolute. A thunderbolt will not come from the heavens and strike you down if you break one of them. And, almost certainly, everyone has at one time or another broken each of the rules.

However, they are more than guidelines. They do need to be followed to get the best results. If you do transgress one of them, we want you to feel guilty, admit to your sins and work out how you will avoid doing something so terrible ever again.

But do remember that if the band is not correctly adjusted you will not be able to follow the rules. You must be in the green zone (see Chapter 9) to follow them. So, before being consumed by self-loathing at your weakness, do consider whether correcting the adjustment of the band is needed and come in to talk to us about it.

We have already discussed these rules in the preceding chapters. In this chapter the rules are restated as a condensation of the advice in the earlier chapters.

We repeat the key elements of the advice. We state the rules and briefly expand on what each rule intends. If you are unsure about what they mean, reread Chapters 7 to 9 on eating, exercise and adjustment and, if still unclear, talk to us.

We have also prepared a DVD of the eight golden rules and attached it to your copy of this book. The DVD is independently important for two reasons. Firstly, it is sometimes easier to learn when you see and hear someone teaching than when you read what they have written. As we consider these rules to be critically important to achieving an optimal outcome, the better we teach them, the better you will be able to fulfill your part of the partnership.

Secondly, and perhaps more importantly, we are able to provide on the DVD some important video animations that illustrate some things in a way that a book cannot. They show how food is meant to be squeezed across the region of the band, how the band works by getting signals from the compression of the band and the squeezing past of the food and how eating too fast or too big a bite can stretch the area above the band and hurt the outcome. In providing a graphic picture of what is happening, these animations have proved to be very helpful to people with a band.

THE EIGHT GOLDEN RULES

1   Eat three or less small meals per day.

2   Do not eat anything between meals.

3   Eat slowly and stop when no longer hungry.

4   Focus on nutritious foods.

5   Avoid calorie-containing liquids.

6   Exercise for at least 30 minutes every day.

7   Be active throughout each day.

8   Always keep in contact with us.

1 EAT THREE OR LESS SMALL MEALS PER DAY

There are two parts to this rule. Eat three or less meals per day and eat small meals. We will discuss them separately. Remember that the LAP-BAND™ works primarily by taking away your appetite. If it is adjusted correctly you should not feel hungry. You may eat up to three times a day. But we don't mind if you eat less often. In fact, we are pleased if you only wish for two meals or even one meal per day. After the band it is very common for people not to feel like breakfast. And some will miss a midday meal. If you don't feel inclined to eat, don't eat. If, on the other hand, you find you are getting hungry between meals, tell us. We will probably consider adjusting the band a little tighter.

The second part is to eat small meals. You don't need a big plate of food. You need the amount of food that could be compressed into half a glass. That is about 125 mL of food. Note that half a glass is a concept and not a measure. The idea is of compressed food. For food like fish or eggs, it is a straight measure. But recognize that vegetables contain a lot of air and water, and allow for that. Fruit is mostly water. And sugar, also, so be wary.

Use a small plate and a small fork or spoon. Take small bites. Chew the food well. Chew it until it is mush. There should be no lumps. If you cannot reduce a bite of food to mush, don't swallow it. Spit it out. Chewing the food well provides an excellent opportunity for enjoying the food—its tastes, textures and flavors. You should be able to enjoy food even more after the band for this reason. It encourages you to enjoy the tastes of the food. You are reducing the quantity, but not the quality.

2 DO NOT EAT ANYTHING BETWEEN MEALS

No snacks, no cookies or biscuits with your coffee, no fruit, nothing. All food must be restricted to mealtimes. One of the most frequent causes for failure is the taking of snacks between meals. If you are getting hungry between meals and are tempted to have a snack, you must tell us. It is probably due to inadequate adjustment and you may need more fluid added to the band. Between meals you can have as much zero-calorie liquids as you wish—water, mineral water, tea, coffee or low-calorie soft drinks.

If you are going to break this rule, if you are really getting hungry and cannot come in for an adjustment for a few days, eat something reasonably healthy. Don't buy the chocolate bar. Try some raw vegetables, such as

a few slices of bell pepper (capsicum), some radishes, crisp lettuce or maybe some fruit. A few almonds or other nuts are about as close to the fault line as I would like you to get. And come in to see us urgently.

3 EAT SLOWLY AND STOP WHEN NO LONGER HUNGRY

Eat slowly. This is the most important of all the rules. You have probably never eaten slowly in your life. It is tough. It takes concentration. It takes training. But you must eat slowly. Firstly, chew well. Enjoy the food and create the mush. Then swallow and wait. Allow 1 minute from one swallow to the next. One minute is a long time. But we know it may take you up to 1 minute for a bite of food to pass across the band completely. We described this on pages 148–149. It is essential that each bite goes completely through the band before you have another bite. You will not know that it has gone across. You must wait for that minute to pass. You can take another bite before the minute is up but don't swallow it—chew it and enjoy it. Then, after the minute from the last swallow, you can swallow it.

Each meal should only last for 20 to 30 minutes. Hopefully 20 minutes, but we will accept up to 30 minutes. That is just 20 bites. Barely enough to eat that half a glass of food. Good. I prefer that you do not finish it all. Leave some. That can be the angels' share. Stop eating when you are no longer hungry. Not when you are full. I don't want you ever to feel full. To get that full feeling you have to stretch the stomach above the band. We do not want that to happen. Ever. Do not expect to feel full and do not eat looking for that fullness. You have gone too far.

Eat until you are no longer hungry. Every bite of food is squeezed across the band. It may take up to six squeezes per bite. Each squeeze generates signals that pass up to the brain telling it that you are not hungry. A meal of 20 bites and maybe four squeezes per bite has generated around 80 signals to the brain saying you are no longer hungry. Listen for them and acknowledge them. Stop eating. There is no reason to eat if you are not hungry.

4 FOCUS ON NUTRITIOUS FOODS

We do not want you to eat much food, only about the amount you could compress into half a glass. Make sure it is good food, nutritious and flavorsome, food that you can enjoy for its qualities, not the quantity of it. Food that is high in protein (for example, meat, especially fish, eggs, dairy products, lentils, soy, tofu, beans) is preferred. At least half of that half a glass of food should be protein-rich. Food that is high in complex carbohydrates (for example, vegetables, some fruit and cereals) is also encouraged. Simple sugars are worst. Be careful with food that is high in fats, as it is a dense form of calories. Be aware that fruit contains quite a lot of sugar.

The good foods can come from all the main food groups and include meat, vegetables, eggs and dairy. There is no need to focus unduly on the particular foods. It is not rocket science. It is simply selecting food that is good (protein and complex carbohydrates), being careful with those that are not so good (fats, alcohol, starches) and avoiding those that are bad (simple sugars). The small volume of food is, by far, the most important. And take a well-balanced vitamin and mineral replacement each day.

5 AVOID CALORIE-CONTAINING LIQUIDS

We want you to achieve satiety, that state of not being hungry. We need the food to be squeezed past the band

to generate that feeling. Liquids do not do this. With normal adjustment of the band, liquids will tend to flow past the band without giving you any feeling of satiety. You get the calories without getting that state of satiety. You are then more likely to remain hungry and eat too much. You must restrict your fluid intake to zero-calorie liquids only. You are allowed to drink unlimited amounts of:

• water
• mineral water
• tea or coffee (with low-fat milk if you wish, but no sugar)
• low-calorie soft drinks.

The two exceptions to the "no liquid calorie" rule are up to one glass of wine each day with a meal, which we know is good for your health and good for your weight loss when taken in a modest amount, and up to 1 pint (500 mL) of low-fat milk each day.

6 EXERCISE FOR AT LEAST 30 MINUTES EVERY DAY

This is at least as important as all of the other rules. Not only must you take in less calories but you must also use up more calories. Exercise will improve your general health as well. Initially, while you are severely obese, this can be difficult, but, as your weight decreases, it becomes easier. As you become fitter and healthier, you get greater enjoyment from exercise.

We understand that not everybody is sports-minded and exercise may be something quite new for you. Start slowly and seek to build up activity progressively. Aim to put together at least 30 minutes of moderate-intensity physical activity on most and preferably

all days. Aim to build up to 60 minutes per day. Walking is ideal to start off with. As your fitness improves, progress to more vigorous walking and even jogging, cycling, aerobics, swimming, and light resistance training. As your weight comes down your exercise capacity will increase and your general activities during the day will increase. This is to be encouraged, and the more active you are the better the result will be.

Your exercise program should be aerobic. You should be puffing and, if you check your pulse, generally it should be up around 120 beats per minute. A wide range of activities will allow you to achieve this. If you can manage it, a personal trainer or fitness consultant can be an excellent assistant. They can provide an individual program according to your specific preferences

and lifestyle that is realistic and achievable. Regular exercise requires commitment. The more effort you put in, the greater benefits you will see and feel.

7 BE ACTIVE THROUGHOUT EACH DAY

Think of movement and activity as opportunities and not as an inconvenience. Try to be active every day in as many ways as you can. Make it a habit to walk or cycle instead of using the car. Become active in the garden and do things yourself instead of using machines. Avoid sitting down at all cost. You should see sitting down as an opportunity for activity lost.

Try to spend as much time outdoors as possible. We tend to be more active when outdoors. Use a pedometer as a stimulus to show you how your activity level is increasing. If you are using a pedometer, aim to get beyond 10,000 steps per day—this represents a very good level of routine daily activity.

8 ALWAYS KEEP IN CONTACT WITH US

We want to follow you permanently. There will never be a time when we say that the job of controlling your obesity is done and we do not need to see you anymore. There will always be a need to check your progress, monitor your health, check for nutritional deficiencies, make sure that you understand the rules, bring you up to date with new developments, and adjust the volume of fluid in the band.

There will always be a very small loss of fluid from the band over time. For example, if you had 7.0 mL of fluid

present and we checked the volume after a 6-month period, there would probably be about 6.7 mL present. This happens because the balloon of the band is not totally impermeable. If 7.0 mL was the correct volume, you would be starting to get hungry and eat more with a volume of 6.7 mL. It is important you understand that this can happen and come back to see us for replacement of that small fluid loss.

CHAPTER 12

FREQUENTLY ASKED QUESTIONS

SHOULD I EXPECT A LOT OF VOMITING?

There really should be no vomiting at all if you are eating correctly and we have the adjustment right. If you find that you are vomiting, then either there is something wrong with the settings of the band or there is something wrong with your following of the rules about eating. Almost everyone will have occasions when they feel food gets stuck. They eat the wrong food or eat too quickly or fail to chew it properly. You feel it sit there. You hope it will go through but it doesn't. You go to the bathroom and bring it up. It is not really vomiting, more regurgitation. It will happen. But repeated vomiting should not happen. Come in and talk to us about it. Something needs to be corrected. It is important not to have frequent vomiting, as this could lead to shifting of the stomach within the band and compromise the outcome. Ideally, there would be no vomiting at all.

WHAT SHOULD I DO IF I DO GET VOMITING FOR OTHER REASONS?

Of course, you are at risk of having vomiting, just as anyone else might, from food poisoning, gastroenteritis, pregnancy or numerous other reasons. Curiously, it has not proved to be at all common and rarely has it been a problem. Your first task is prevention. Avoid eating or drinking potentially contaminated food or water. This is particularly important when you are traveling. If you start vomiting and feel it may continue, seek medical help to stop it as quickly as possible. If it continues, contact the clinic and have some fluid removed from the band. Once you start vomiting a lot, there is swelling of the stomach inside the band, making it tighter. The swelling perpetuates the vomiting. Removing fluid breaks that cycle.

WILL I BE CONSTIPATED?

You may be. It is inevitable that as you eat less food, you eat less fiber, and your bowel activity will decrease. However, we have been pleasantly surprised to find that this has not proved to be a common problem at all. If you do become constipated, it is acceptable to take one of the bulk-forming laxatives, such as Metamucil, with plenty of water and this should correct the problem.

SHOULD I TAKE A VITAMIN SUPPLEMENT?

Yes. You may well be getting sufficient vitamins from the food that you are able to take, but as you lose weight you have a particular need for additional vitamins and, therefore, we strongly recommend that you do take a multivitamin supplement. It is particularly important that the supplement has sufficient folate and vitamin B12. We will monitor specific vitamins and minerals, such as vitamin B12 and folate and iron, each year after operation to check for any deficiency in these. If there is any deficiency, specific addition will be recommended.

WHAT ABOUT OTHER TABLETS AND MEDICINES?

In general you will continue to take the medications prescribed. However, if they are in the form of a bulky tablet, it may be necessary to break them up. Try them out. If they feel as if they tend to stick at the bottom of the esophagus, you may have to crush them and take them with some yogurt to disguise the taste. However, if you are going to do this, check with your pharmacist first, as quite a number of tablets are specially formulated to be slowly released or released further down the gut and not in the stomach. Capsules should not be a problem to swallow as they are designed to soften and melt inside the body.

WHAT HAPPENS IF I BECOME PREGNANT?

We have now had many pregnancies in our patients and it has been all good news. The band itself does not interfere in any negative way with the pregnancy. The likelihood of becoming pregnant is higher because, having lost weight, your periods are often more regular. The adjustability of the band makes managing the pregnancy much easier, because we can remove some fluid from the band if you have a lot of vomiting early on or if you are not putting on enough weight for you and the baby. Normally, we will adjust the volume of fluid in the band early in the pregnancy to ensure that there is optimal nutritional intake for both yourself and the baby. Even if you put on some weight during the pregnancy, we can tighten it up again later and get that weight off again.

IS THE SILICONE DANGEROUS TO ME?

We have no information to suggest that it is. We have been using silicone implants in various areas of surgery for more than 60 years. There were concerns and a lot of legal actions raised regarding the liquid silicone used in breast implants. However, this turned out to be more of a political and legal rumor than a true medical problem, as a review of a large number of high-quality medical studies was unable to show that what was being claimed was true.

The LAP-BAND™ is made of solid silicone and has no liquid component. Therefore, it cannot leak into the tissues in the way that liquid silicone possibly could. We expect the likelihood of any problem to be extremely low. However, it could be that information about problems relevant to this question may become available in the future. If they do, we would let you know.

HOW LONG WILL THE BAND LAST?

We really don't know. We have been using the LAP-BAND™ for more than 15 years and there has been no sign of it wearing out. However, realistically we can't expect a device such as this to last 40 to 50 years. We do expect that somewhere down the track there will be failure of the adjusting balloon, in particular, and should this occur, the band would need to be replaced. It is going to remain to be determined if and when this should be necessary. We are hopeful that you will get good service from the LAP-BAND™ for at least 20 years and if, after that, we have to replace it, well, so be it.

CAN THE BAND BE REMOVED?

Yes. It can be removed quite easily. It is not our intention to ever remove it, but should it become appropriate for whatever reason, then it can be removed. If it has been placed laparoscopically, then it can be removed laparoscopically. After the band has been removed, we would expect the stomach to go back to normal.

However, if the band was removed and no other effective method for weight control was instituted, we would expect that you would regain the weight that you had lost. It might happen slowly but it is most likely that over a 2-year period you would return to your original weight.

WHAT DO I DO WHEN DINING OUT?

Because of the limited capacity of your new "virtual" stomach, you must restrict yourself generally to an appetizer (an entrée in Australia). Eat slowly while those with you are overeating with two or three courses. Social eating is one setting where we will excuse you from the 20-minute rule. Because these occasions may go on for some hours, we recommend that you pick very slowly at your food over this time. Push it around the plate and nibble at it.

If you are visiting friends, it is probably better to advise the host or hostess that you can only eat a small amount to save embarrassment when you reject most of their carefully prepared food.

WHAT ABOUT ALCOHOL?

Alcohol has a high calorie content and is a liquid and therefore, in theory, should be discouraged. However, there are health advantages to a modest alcohol intake, particularly of wine. And we have found from our research that modest alcohol intake is associated with improved weight loss. We therefore are happy to let you have up to seven standard drinks per week, or an average of one drink per day. Note that this is not a requirement; it is the upper limit.

WILL I NEED PLASTIC SURGERY FOR EXCESS SKIN FOLDS ONCE I HAVE LOST WEIGHT?

Generally, no. About a quarter of our patients need to have something done. The most common need is for the removal of the abdominal apron. Generally, we don't want you to consider any plastic surgery until about 2 years after the procedure. Usually there is enough elasticity in the skin to take up the slack sufficiently and we would like to wait to see how effective this is before considering plastic surgery.

WHAT SHOULD HAPPEN IF I DEVELOP ANOTHER ILLNESS?

A real advantage with the gastric band is its adjustability. If you have some other illness that makes it inappropriate to have restriction on food intake, then the fluid can easily be removed and there would be very little limitation on nutrition. Once you have recovered from the illness, even if you have put on weight, the fluid can be added and the original status restored. However, there is no need to remove fluid from the band before an anesthetic. As no solid or liquid food is held up above the band for more than a minute, there is no risk of aspiration as you go under the anesthetic after a 4-hour fast. Reassure your anesthesiologist of this. Show this page to him or her.

CAN I BURP WITH THE LAP-BAND™?

Not so easily. As we eat, we always swallow air and normally we bring this back up again quite unconsciously. The band interferes with this easy bringing up of wind. It is common in the first few weeks after the procedure for people to notice a difficulty with bloating and the feeling that they want to burp but cannot. This rarely seems to persist as a problem months later. We presume that the stomach below the band changes its shape enough to reduce the problem, but for whatever reason it does not seem to continue to be troublesome.

HOW ARE THE ADJUSTMENTS TO THE BAND DONE?

We generally will start tightening the band at 4 weeks after the initial operation. The adjustment is almost always performed in the office at the time of consultation. It does not require any anesthetic. It consists of passing a fine needle through the skin into the access port. It only takes a few minutes to do and is not usually associated with significant discomfort. On occasions it will need to be performed in the radiology department where we can see more accurately where the access port is.

We will generally adjust the band every 2 weeks until we feel that we have the right setting. This may take four or five adjustments. Once the correct setting is reached we would leave it at that level as long as the rate of weight loss initially, and then the weight maintenance later on, was satisfactory. Additional adjustments can be made whenever necessary. When you reach the goal weight, we leave the setting at that level so as to maintain that weight. If we reduced the setting at this time you would expect to find an increase in your weight.

ARE THE ADJUSTMENTS VERY PAINFUL?

No, they are not. Some people worry more about the adjustments before they are done than they worried about the operation. This is really quite inappropriate. Each adjustment consists of a jab with a needle and then some mild discomfort as we push on the access port. It usually only takes 2 or 3 minutes and doesn't require any local anesthetic. It would hurt as much to have the local anesthetic put in as it does to have the whole adjustment. After you have your first adjustment you will be reassured and no longer need to worry.

IS THIS COSMETIC SURGERY?

No. It is not. Obesity is a potentially severe and, in fact, a life-threatening disease, and this procedure is for treatment of this disease. The disease is present when the BMI is greater than 30. It is recognized as such by your health funds and by governmental agencies involved in health. While there are undoubted benefits to your appearance with weight loss, the primary reason for us doing the procedure is the health benefit.

WHAT HAPPENS IF I GO OVERSEAS OR TO REMOTE LOCATIONS?

Generally, there is no problem. You really don't want to get into any difficulties while away and therefore you have to be doubly careful to follow the rules regarding the types of food you eat. Take this book with you and, should you need any medical care while traveling, this will give the physicians elsewhere much of the information that they would need to understand what has been done. We would hope that they would telephone us and discuss the problem before they interfered in any way with the device.

IS AIRPLANE TRAVEL A PROBLEM?

It can be more difficult to eat when flying. There are often little bubbles of air in the balloon of the band. We try to flush these out when we initially prime the band but we cannot clear them all. Generally, they don't matter. However, when you are at 35,000 feet in a plane that is only partially pressurized, these bubbles may expand enough to make the band tighter. You may find that you have difficulty with solid foods and even with liquids. If so, just relax and enjoy the trip. Watch the movie instead of having lunch. When you return to ground level, the bubbles will shrink down and you will be back to normal.

ARE THERE AGE LIMITS FOR THE LAP-BAND?

At the moment the lowest age we would consider is 14 years. We have published a high-quality trial in adolescents, 14–18 years of age, and been able to show a very clear advantage for those who were in the banding group compared with those in the medical treatment group.[14] We are therefore prepared to consider anyone who is obese and who fulfils the other criteria as discussed on pages 114–118. However, I should warn that we move fairly slowly in making a decision with young people, as we need to be sure that both they and their parents know what is involved.

We have no strict upper age limit but, as people exceed the age of 65, we tend to have reduced enthusiasm for the procedure. There are two reasons for us becoming increasingly hesitant. Firstly, the risk of the procedure increases progressively with age. Heart disease and other key health problems are more likely; and although they may not yet be causing symptoms, they do add risk to surgery. Secondly, the rate of weight loss is lower in older people. The weight has often been there a long time and does not move as readily. Therefore, we become less enthusiastic as the risks of LAP-BAND™ surgery get higher and the benefits get lower. For all that, however, we have treated a few people over 70 with good results. It may be worth a chat and a health assessment.

REFERENCES

1. Yach D, Stuckler D, Brownell K. Epidemiologic and economic consequences of the global epidemics of obesity and diabetes. *Nat Med* 2006; 12(1):62–66.
2. Mokdad AH, Marks JS, Stroup DF, Gerberding JL. Actual causes of death in the United States, 2000. *JAMA* 2004; 291(10):1238–1245.
3. Flegal KM, Graubard BI, Williamson DF, Gail MH. Excess deaths associated with underweight, overweight, and obesity. *JAMA* 2005; 293(15): 1861–1867.
4. Colditz GA, Willett WC, Rotnitzky A, Manson JE. Weight gain as a risk factor for clinical diabetes mellitus in women. *Ann Intern Med* 1995; 122(7): 481–486.
5. Dixon JB, O'Brien PE, Playfair J, Chapman L, Schachter LM, Skinner S, Proietto J, Bailey M, Anderson M. Adjustable gastric banding and conventional therapy for type 2 diabetes: a randomized controlled trial. *JAMA* 2008; 299(3):316-23.
6. O'Brien PE, Brown WA, Dixon JB. Obesity, weight loss and bariatric surgery. *Med J Aust* 2005; 183(6):310–314.
7. Dixon JB, Dixon ME, O'Brien PE. Birth outcomes in obese women after laparoscopic adjustable gastric banding. *Obstet Gynecol* 2005; 106(5): 965–72.

8. Peeters A, O'Brien PE, Laurie C, Anderson M, Wolfe R, Flum D, et al. Substantial intentional weight loss and mortality in the severely obese. *Ann Surg* 2007; 246(6): 1028–33.

9. Glenny AM, O'Meara S, Melville A, Sheldon TA, Wilson C. The treatment and prevention of obesity: a systematic review of the literature. *Int J Obes Relat Metab Disord* 1997; 21(9):715–737.

10. Li Z, Maglione M, Tu W, et al. Meta-analysis: pharmacologic treatment of obesity. *Ann Intern Med* 2005; 142(7):532–546.

11. O'Brien PE, McPhail T, Chaston TB, Dixon JB. Systemic review of medium term weight loss after bariatric operations. *Obes Surg* 2006; 16(8): 1032–1040.

12. Chapman A, Kiroff G, Game P, et al. Laparoscopic adjustable gastric banding in the treatment of obesity: a systematic review. *Surgery* 2004; 135: 326–351.

13. O'Brien PE, Dixon J, Laurie C, et al. Treatment of mild to moderate obesity with laparoscopic adjustable gastric banding or an intensive medical program: a randomized trial. *Ann Intern Med* 2006; 144:625–633.

14. O'Brien PE, Sawyer SM, Laurie C, Brown WA, Skinner S, Veit F, et al. Laparoscopic adjustable gastric banding in severely obese adolescents: a randomized trial. *JAMA* 2010; 303(6): 519–26.

INDEX

(Note: Page numbers in bold indicate figure)